PEARSON
Revise

T0346001

Pearson Edexcel GCSE (9–1)

History

Migrants in Britain, c800–present

Revision Guide and Workbook

Series Consultant: Harry Smith

Authors: Rosemary Rees and Ben Armstrong

A note from the publisher

In order to ensure that this resource offers high-quality support for the associated Pearson qualification, it has been through a review process by the awarding body. This process confirms that this resource fully covers the teaching and learning content of the specification or part of a specification at which it is aimed. It also confirms that it demonstrates an appropriate balance between the development of subject skills, knowledge and understanding, in addition to preparation for assessment.

Endorsement does not cover any guidance on assessment activities or processes (e.g. practise questions or advice on how to answer assessment questions), included in the resource nor does it prescribe any particular approach to the teaching or delivery of a related course.

While the publishers have made every attempt to ensure that advice on the qualification and its assessment is accurate, the official specification and associated assessment guidance materials are the only authoritative source of information and should always be referred to for definitive guidance.

Pearson examiners have not contributed to any sections in this resource relevant to examination papers for which they have responsibility.

Examiners will not use endorsed resources as a source of material for any assessment set by Pearson.

Endorsement of a resource does not mean that the resource is required to achieve this Pearson qualification, nor does it mean that it is the only suitable material available to support the qualification, and any resource lists produced by the awarding body shall include this and other appropriate resources.

Contents

. . . .

A small bit of small print

Pearson Edexcel publishes Sample Assessment Material and the Specification on its website. This is the official content and this book should be used in conjunction with it. The questions in *Now try this* have been written to help you practise every topic in the book. Remember: the real exam questions may not look like this.

Note: The Migrants in Britain thematic study aims to help make the study of History more diverse and inclusive. It is an important topic which looks at attitudes to different groups of people at different points in time and over time. Views on race and the language used to discuss these views have changed over time. Some words used commonly in the past – such as 'coloured', used to refer to black people – are now widely recognised as offensive. While we condemn racism, we think it is important to report these attitudes both for historical accuracy and in order that we can learn from them, and this is reflected in some of the sources chosen for this Revision Guide.

Medieval England

Medieval England in the 9th century was one of the wealthiest countries in northern Europe. It was an inviting prospect for raiders, invaders and settlers.

The nature of medieval England and English society in the 9th century

England had rich mineral deposits of lead and iron, copper, tin and silver. These were used to construct buildings and to make tools, weapons, jewellery and other objects.

Fertile land, especially in the east and south, meant crops grew well. Sheep produced high-quality wool essential for cloth-making. There were plentiful supplies of salt to preserve meat for the winter; and the rivers and seas were full of fish.

The Anglo-Saxon kingdoms of 9th-century England

Trade routes inland and with Europe were well established. Anglo-Saxon merchants traded in large quantities of various goods. For example, they exported cheese, wool, cloth and minerals, and imported glass, wine, silks and spices.

Most people lived in villages, but fortified towns (called burhs or burgs) grew in number and developed as trading centres, especially those that were on the coast or navigable rivers.

Many monasteries and abbeys were extremely wealthy, owning hundreds of gold and silver objects, precious jewels and beautifully illustrated manuscripts.

Christianity

In the early medieval period, England gradually adopted Christianity. By 1066, it was a Christian country. Monasteries that were branches of European monastic orders were built. Scholars and clergy moved freely between England and Europe as England became part of Christendom.

The Church and Christendom

Christianity was brought to England by the Romans. When the Roman army left Britain in 410, Christianity was still simply one religion among many. Then change came.

563: Irish Christian missionaries founded an abbey on the island of Iona, in Scotland.

597: The pope sent Augustine, a Christian missionary, from Rome to England. This increased the spread of Christianity.

635: Christian missionaries from Iona founded an abbey at Lindisfarne, on Holy Island, off the coast of Northumbria.

Government

- Anglo-Saxon people were originally divided into many small kingdoms. Gradually, after much fighting, larger kingdoms emerged.
- The most important kingdoms in the 9th century were Northumbria, Mercia, Wessex, Kent and East Anglia.
- Kings had the ultimate authority in their own kingdoms. They were usually advised by groups of the most powerful men in their kingdom. These could be a mixture of land-owning nobles and churchmen.
- Money to run the kingdoms was raised by taxation based on land ownership.
- Law and order were maintained by local communities who were responsible for preventing crime and catching criminals.
- The lack of a central government meant that it was difficult to organise a defence against invaders.

Athelstan was the first king of all England. He reigned from 925 to 939.

Key term

✓ **Christendom**: All the countries where Christianity was the main religion.

Now try this

Give **three** reasons why England was attractive to people wanting to invade and settle in the 9th century.

Migration and settlement

Vikings, Normans, Jews and other Europeans migrated to medieval England for many different reasons. However, all migrants were attracted by England's wealth and resources.

Vikings

From c789 to c865 Vikings raided England and Scotland, attacking villages and towns and monasteries and abbeys that were close to the coast. They did this because they wanted the treasure held in monasteries and abbeys; the goods stored in merchants' warehouses; the ransoms they could demand to return captured people.

In 865 the Viking Great Army landed in East Anglia. The Vikings now wanted to settle in England because they knew the fertile soils would provide the land they needed.

In 866 Vikings captured York and used it as a base for defeating Northumbria, East Anglia and Mercia.

In 878 Alfred of Wessex (the one remaining Saxon kingdom) and Guthrum, leader of the Vikings, agreed the Treaty of Wedmore. This established that the Viking migrants now controlled a large part of England and ran it using their own laws.

This was called the **Danelaw**.

Normans

The Normans, from Normandy in northern France, invaded England in 1066. Led by Duke William they wanted to conquer and rule England their way because:

- They believed William had been promised the English throne by both Edward the Confessor and Harold Godwinson. However, on Edward's death, Harold became king.
- They received the support of the pope, who backed the invasion because of what he believed were broken promises.
- England's wealth, fertile soil and trading links made it an attractive place to settle.

In 1066, at the Battle of Hastings, William and his Norman army defeated Harold Godwinson's Saxon army. William was crowned king of England on Christmas Day 1066.

Norman nobles and merchants then migrated to England to gain land and to take advantage of the trade routes developed by the Saxons and the Vikings.

Jews

William I's plans for England involved spending a great deal of money, mainly on building castles and cathedrals. Christians did not generally lend money because, under Church rules, they were not allowed to charge interest. William turned to Jewish people in Normandy from whom he had previously borrowed money. Jews were allowed to charge interest on loans.

A group of Jewish merchants decided to lend William the money he wanted. In 1070, invited by William, they arrived in London, and were given 'special status' as 'the property of the king'. Their families soon followed and established a small community in the city.

Charging interest was called **usury** and was regarded as a sin by the Catholic Church.

Skilled workers from Europe

Workers migrated to England because:

The Hundred Years' War disrupted work and trade, especially in France. However, England was a stable country where workers with skills could do well.

The Black Death killed 30% to 40% of England's population in the years 1348–51. As a result, there was plenty of both skilled and unskilled work available in England as well as the chance to set up new businesses.

Henry III wanted to replace Jewish moneylenders with Christians because anti-Semitic attitudes were becoming common. So he invited powerful Italian banking families to England. In the 1220s the Bardi and Ricciardi families moved to London to work as bankers under royal protection.

Now try this

List **four** reasons for medieval migration. Then note down to which group(s) each reason applies – Vikings, Normans, Jews, European workers and/or Italian bankers.

Migrants: Experience

The experience of migrants in England c800–c1500 depended very much on the skills they brought, what their ambitions were and how they were seen by the existing population.

The experience of the Vikings

Most Vikings led settled lives in the Danelaw. They set up their own shops, markets and workshops, built their own houses and enjoyed their own forms of entertainment. Some grew rich because of the trading links developed with Europe.

Relations between the Vikings and the Saxons were generally good. However, for settled Vikings (known as Danes) living near the boundary of the Danelaw, fighting the Saxons was an everyday experience.

Relations became worse after the Danelaw was brought under Saxon control in 937. The Danes began raiding again and Viking settlers were sometimes attacked by Saxons.

Eventually, in 1016, Cnut became the first Danish king of England. Relations improved, at least partly because Cnut set up new earldoms, giving a few Saxon nobles very large areas of land.

The experience of the Normans

After 1066 the Normans had to establish their control over England.

- Most Normans regularly experienced hostility and resentment from the Saxons. This was due partly to the cruelty with which the Norman army crushed rebellions in the West Country, East Anglia and the north of England. Another reason was that the Saxons were forced to build castles for the Normans, sometimes having to destroy large areas of towns.

- The feudal system ensured that the Normans, as barons, bishops and knights, held positions of authority over the Saxons.

- Land in England was now totally owned by the king. He kept some for himself, gave some to the Church, and then shared most of the rest with Norman nobles who were loyal to him. They knew the value of the land they were taking over because of the Domesday Book. They also knew what crops would grow and which animals would do well.

Made sure they were kept safe by lending money to monarchs who protected them in return, allowing them to shelter in castles during dangerous times.

Were well-respected in local communities for many years because of the financial support they gave to small businesses.

Increasingly experienced anti-Semitism as people began to resent paying interest on loans. Interest rates were high to cover the taxes Jews had to pay.

Jewish migrants

The 1275 Statute of Jewry made Jews wear a yellow armband. It also meant Jews were forbidden from charging interest on loans. Many Jews became desperately poor.

In 1290 Jews were expelled from England by Edward I.

Key term

 Anti-Semitism is the term to describe prejudice and discrimination against Jewish people.

Migrants from Europe

Flemish weavers had specialised skills that English weavers didn't have. They were welcomed because they taught their skills to the English weavers and helped the cloth trade to flourish and employment to increase.

Hansa merchants from Germany were given the right to trade in England by Edward I. They set up the Steelyard in London, from which they directed and controlled trade with the Hanseatic League and other parts of Europe. By the mid-1400s, German merchants controlled most of the English cloth industry.

Lombardy bankers – from 1220 there were powerful Italian banking families working in London. They did well, especially after the expulsion of Jewish people in 1290 and even after Edward III stopped repaying their loans.

In difficult times, the English people turned on migrants. For example, during the Peasants' Revolt in 1381, about 150 migrants were murdered and the Hansa Steelyard was burned down. Craft guilds regularly complained that 'foreigners' were taking work from them.

Now try this

List **four** problems faced by migrants as they tried to settle in England. Name the migrant group each time.

Migrants: Impact

Migrants had a huge impact on English society c800–c1500, especially on government, the Church, trade, the built environment and the economy.

Government

Migrants changed and developed the way England was governed:

- **Vikings** in the Danelaw introduced *Things*, where members voted on laws. *Things* were also law courts and members agreed on a punishment for those they found guilty.
- **Normans** developed the Saxon system of government into an established parliament with lords and commons.

When migrants ruled, they introduced new laws that had an impact on everyone. For example:

- **Forest Laws** created royal forests where the king controlled who could hunt.
- The Normans also introduced the '**murdrum**' which was a fine paid by Saxons if a Norman was murdered and the culprit wasn't found.

There were also new laws that were specific to migrants. For example:

- **1370:** Letters of denization gave individual migrants the same rights as English people.
- **1440:** Parliament levied a tax on 'aliens', defined legally as first-generation migrants.

The impact of the Normans on the Church

- The Normans built thousands of churches, cathedrals and monasteries. The construction of many religious buildings was financed by loans from Jewish migrants.
- Since the Church was so important in daily life, the clergy had more power and influence.
- The number of monks and nuns increased 400% between 1066 and 1500.
- Church organisation became more hierarchical, with parish priests at the bottom and archbishops at the top. This drew the English Church more firmly into Christendom.
- Saxon bishops and archbishops were removed and replaced by Normans.

The impact of migrants in medieval England

The built environment

- Viking raids led the Saxons to develop burhs (burgs) – **fortified towns**.
- Normans built **castles** and **cathedrals** from **stone** and replaced wooden **churches** with stone ones.
- **Towns**, mainly in East Anglia, grew and developed because the Flemish weavers settled there.
- **Ports** grew, especially London and Kings Lynn, building wharves and warehouses because of the Hansa merchants (traders from Germany).

Culture

- **New words** crept into the **language**, e.g. 'skill' and 'husband' (Norse), 'comfort' and 'leisure' (French), and 'kosher' and 'synagogue' (Jewish). Gradually, Norman French and Saxon English came together as Middle English, although French was the official language until 1362.
- The feudal system changed **land ownership** and **obligations and duties** between people in different levels of society. Under the Saxons, the king was one of a small number of landowners but after the Norman invasion the king owned all land in England. He granted it to those who were loyal to him.

Trade

| **Weavers:** Skilled weavers wove high-quality, fine woollen cloth that merchants exported to Europe, where it was in high demand. England's economy changed from being based on raw materials (wool) to one based on manufactured goods (cloth). | → | **Merchants:** Merchants traded goods in Europe, particularly with Hansa merchants. They grew rich and invested their money in banks and began to turn England into a key trading centre. | → | **Bankers:** Lombardy bankers in turn loaned money to finance trade and to help pay for buildings such as castles, warehouses and banks. They also lent money to monarchs for military campaigns. They began to turn London into a financial hub. |

See page 5 for information on how the Vikings helped trade develop.

Now try this

Describe **one** similarity and **one** difference in how the Vikings and Normans made an impact on England.

York under the Vikings

Case study In 866 the Vikings captured the city of York. They turned it into a great multicultural and prosperous city – thousands of merchants and skilled migrants worked there, creating trading links with Europe, Russia and North Africa.

Reasons why the Vikings made a settlement at York

← The Vikings named the city Jorvik.

1. It was the centre of Anglo-Saxon government in the north and had the only mint in northern England.
2. It was surrounded by fertile land.
3. It had good trade routes inland and overseas.
4. Viking raiders often targeted York because of its wealth.
5. The Vikings conquered Northumbria, capturing York first in 866 and finally in 867.

York grew under the Vikings. The Anglo-Saxon population was about 1,000. Between 867 and 950, 10,000–15,000 people migrated to York.

Hundreds of houses and workshops were built, as well as warehouses and wharves along the river Ouse.

York became a multicultural city. As well as Scandinavia, migrants came from Germany, the Netherlands, Ireland and Scotland. Anglo-Saxons and Vikings migrated from other parts of England.

York: The impact of the Vikings

Skilled migrants worked on many different trades. There were, for example, clothworkers and woodturners, jewellery-makers and metalworkers, potters, blacksmiths and glassmakers.

Trade flourished. Merchants used the old Roman roads for moving goods inland. The River Ouse was the route to the North Sea and trade with European ports and cities.

The Vikings and the Church

- The Vikings kept the stone Saxon church in York, later called York Minster; other churches were built in Viking settlements outside York.
- In 939 Archbishop Wulfstan negotiated a border between the Vikings and Anglo-Saxons.
- Many coins minted in York had a Christian symbol on one side, linking trade with Christianity.
- Many Viking kings converted to Christianity and King Guthrum was buried in York minster.

For more on King Guthrum, see page 2.

The migrants' influence on York remained long after Viking rule ended.

Relations with the Anglo-Saxons

Inside York, Saxons and Vikings generally lived peacefully. It was different for their rulers, however, and fighting was common.

Timeline

867 Saxons tried to push Vikings out of York and failed.

939 Vikings recaptured York, which they held until 954 when the Saxons took over again.

For information on Athelstan, see page 1.

927 Athelstan conquered large parts of the Viking kingdom of York and the city.

1016–35 King Cnut ruled the whole of England

Think about the link between trade and the skilled migrants settling in York.

Now try this

Explain **three** of the links between the five 'legs' of the concept map 'York: The impact of the Vikings'.

Had a look ☐   Nearly there ☐   Nailed it! ☐

Early modern England

The period c1500–c1700 was one of tremendous change in England and English society. These changes – to social structures, the economy and trade, and religion – affected nearly everyone.

Changes in government

Parliament met more regularly in the 1500s and began to want a greater say in government. This led to clashes with the monarch as Parliament tried to limit the powers of the Crown.

Timeline

1649 Execution of Charles I.

1660 Parliament invited Charles I's son to reign as Charles II, but limited his powers.

1688 Parliament asked Protestant William of Orange to invade England; he became William III and ruled jointly with his wife Mary, the Protestant daughter of James II.

1642–51 Civil war between Charles I and Parliament – Parliament won.

1649–60 England was a republic, for most of the time led by Oliver Cromwell.

1685 James II became king; his Catholicism made him unpopular.

1689 William and Mary signed the Bill of Rights which increased the power of parliament; this meant those who elected MPs had a greater influence on government – a huge change to the social structure of England.

Changes in religion

At the start of the 1500s, England was a Catholic country. Then everything changed.

Henry VIII (1509–47) remained a Catholic, but in 1534 he became head of the Church in England (whereas previously the pope had been the head). This brought huge changes to society – monasteries and nunneries were abolished; monks and nuns had to look for other work; and the poor had nowhere to go for help.

⬇

Edward VI (1547–53) changed England into a Protestant country.

⬇

Mary 1 (1553–58) turned England back into a Catholic country.

⬇

Elizabeth I (1558–1603) changed England into a fully Protestant country where the pope had no power.

Key term

✓ **Protestants**: Christians who disagreed with the teachings of the Catholic Church and set up their own Church(es).

Privateers were sailors licensed by a government to attack enemy ships and take the goods they carried.

Factors bringing about change

Religion	Economic growth	Government
England became a Protestant country, free from the power of the pope. European Protestants, especially Huguenots, saw England as a place of safety. They brought wealth and new ideas to England.	Global trading companies developed routes to Africa, Europe and India. Privateering increased. Merchants traded in a wide range of goods, and the cloth trade dominated England's prosperity. The transatlantic slave trade began, taking people from Africa and selling them into slavery in the Caribbean (also known as the West Indies) and America.	Parliament passed laws that encouraged migrants to settle in England. New laws supported the growth of trade and set up trading companies. Jews, who had been expelled in 1290, were allowed to return by Oliver Cromwell and the Protectorate.

See page 7 for more on Huguenots.

See page 3 for the expulsion of Jews from England.

Now try this

Give **two** ways in which England became more attractive to migrants during these years.

Migration and settlement

Some of the reasons for migration in this period were the same as in earlier periods. Others were different. As before, many came to England to trade and prosper while others saw England as a refuge from persecution. However, not all migrants travelled willingly.

Migrants to Protestant England

Huguenot migrants

- They were Protestants who left France in two main periods (1550–72 and 1670–1710) because they were persecuted by the Catholic authorities. Edward VI allowed a French Protestant Church to be founded in London in 1550. Charles II offered them denizen status in 1681, which allowed migrants to live in England with certain rights.
- Many were skilled craftworkers. They wanted to set up businesses and trade, and many settled in areas where relatives had already become successful.

The Foreign Protestants Nationality Act (1709) allowed European Protestants full civil rights in Britain provided they swore loyalty to the Crown.

Palatine migrants

- They were mostly Protestant farmers who left Germany in 1709 because of bad harvests, famine, poverty, and war. They wanted a better life.
- Many were on their way to America, encouraged by the British-owned Carolina Company and funded by the British government.
- They were very poor and had few skills apart from farming and labouring.

Migrants arrived in England from many countries.

GERMAN SHIP OF THE XVI. CENTURY. *From a drawing by Holbein, in the Model Institut, Frankfort.*

Note that you could also use the Palatine refugees as an example in a question about the period c1700–c1900.

Indian migrants

- Increased trade took English people to India where Indian men worked in clerical jobs and Indian women worked as servants to English families.
- Some Indians, especially ayahs (nannies) returned to England with the families they worked for and continued working for them.
- Some Indians worked on the ships sailing between England and India, and many settled in English ports, looking for a better way of life.

Sailors from India and south-east Asia were known as lascars.

African migrants

- Africans had lived in England since Roman times, but hundreds migrated to England during this period.
- Many were forced out of Spain in 1568 because they were part of a rebellion against the Spanish government.
- Others had been enslaved but escaped and fled to England.
- Some who had been enslaved were brought into England by their owners.

Jews

- Some Jews remained in England even after they were expelled in 1290. Outwardly, they converted to Christianity but privately followed their faith.
- By the 1650s, Jews were facing increasing anti-Semitism and persecution in Europe.

For more on the expulsion of Jews in 1290, see page 3.

- The English economy was weak. Allowing Jews to return would encourage successful Jewish merchants to migrate. Their expertise could strengthen the economy.
- In 1656, Cromwell allowed Jews to return.

'Gypsies'

- Romani (also known as 'Gypsies') were nomadic people who travelled throughout England and Europe.
- English governments regarded them as vagrants and beggars and passed laws to make them stay in one place.
- Most Romani ignored the laws because their lifestyle made it hard for them to comply. Hundreds were hanged as a punishment.
- In the 1650s the government began transporting Romani people into slavery in North America and the Caribbean.

Now try this

Write a paragraph describing the changes in reasons for migration in early modern England compared with medieval England.

Migrants: Experience

Migrants had mixed experiences in England in the period c1500–c1700. If their skills were seen as useful to the country's economy, they were welcomed and often prospered. However, anti-Semitism grew again, and some of the existing population resented all migrants, partly because they believed the migrants were taking jobs that belonged to them.

Huguenots

- Most had a range of skills and so found work easily and prospered.
- Some worked with friends or relatives who were already established in England.
- Many set up their own businesses.
- Some were desperately poor, and some took to petty crime – as did thousands of English people.
- Occasionally there were riots (for example 1517 May Day riots in London) by people who resented foreigners' privileges.

See pages 7 and 11 for more on Huguenots.

Palatines

- Most had very few skills; a few found labouring work.
- Most relied on charities to live as they had no friends or relatives in England.
- The government was no longer willing to fund emigration to America.
- The government deported thousands to Ireland to work on the land – but this only worked where landowners, for example in Wexford, were supportive.
- About two-thirds of those deported drifted back to England. Many sailed to America but few survived.

Note that you could also use the Palatine refugees as an example in a question about the period c1700–c1900.

Mixed migrant experiences, c1500–c1700

Jews

- The first Jews to return to England after their expulsion in 1290 settled in London. Here, the authorities gave them permission to open a synagogue.
- They worked mainly as bankers, doctors, scholars and jewellers.
- Poorer Jews began to migrate from Eastern Europe and usually settled in their arrival ports, working as dockers, traders and pawnbrokers.
- Gradually, Jews settled in most towns and cities in England.
- Poor and destitute Jews were looked after by their own communities.

Indians

- Ayahs' experiences depended very much on their employers. Ayahs lived with the English families who they had worked for in India. When the children grew up, ayahs were either passed on to other wealthy English families to look after their children, or they were abandoned.
- Lascars settled in the ports of London, Liverpool, Glasgow and Cardiff. They worked on the docks, in warehouses and pubs. For many this meant a life of hard labour.

An engraving of lascars.

Anti-Semitism

- Jews were forbidden to serve in the army, work as lawyers or attend universities.
- Jews were described as thieves and scoundrels in popular songs and pamphlets.
- Shylock is a character in the play *The Merchant of Venice*, written in this period. Shylock is Jewish and is portrayed by Shakespeare as a mean and greedy moneylender.

Africans

- Some black Africans who had been enslaved overseas were brought back to England as servants.
- Africans often worked as servants to the wealthy. It was fashionable for rich English people to have a black servant, especially a child.
- Africans were also employed in a variety of skilled jobs, for example, as interpreters, and were paid the same wages as others. They were respected and equal members of society. Some black African migrants became quite wealthy.

John Blanke, African migrant and trumpeter for Henry VIII.

Now try this

Who settled more successfully – Huguenots or Palatines? Give **two** reasons why this was.

Migrants: Impact

Migrants had a tremendous impact on England in the 16th and 17th centuries.

Cloth trade: Boosted by skilled Huguenot silk weavers. Between 1650 and 1700 cloth exports were 20 times greater than between 1600 and 1650.

Maritime trade: Jewish traders working in England's ports helped the growth of Britain's maritime empire.

Finance: Jewish financiers invested in businesses, enabling economic growth and helping turn London into a major financial centre. The first governor of the Bank of England (founded 1694) was a Huguenot, as were 7 of the 25 directors. They created a 'National Debt' that meant governments could borrow large amounts of money for various enterprises.

Impact on trade, industry and finance

Manufacturing industries: Huguenots invested in the Sheffield steel industry and started the English paper industry.

Fashion industry: Silks and new fabrics, such as velvet and taffeta, were in demand by rich women and dress designers.

Huguenots attending Huguenot churches were seen to be respectable because of the similarities with English Protestantism. This helped religious toleration.

Agriculture: the Dutch

In **1630** Charles I asked Cornelius Vermuyden to drain the Fens, in the east of England.

⬇

Dutch engineers and labourers worked for 20 years digging ditches, straightening rivers, and building pumps and windmills.

⬇

By **1642** about 40,000 acres had been turned into fertile farmland.

⬇

New jobs in agriculture were created and landowners became rich.

Draining the Fens meant that some people would lose their jobs cutting rushes, and trapping waterbirds and eels. This meant that some people who lived in the Fens were angry. They were called the Fen Tigers and they attacked and destroyed dams and pumps.

Cornelius Vermuyden was a Dutch engineer employed to drain the Fens. He became an English citizen in 1633.

Culture

Hans Holbein's portrait of Nicholas Kratzer, a German migrant. He was Henry VIII's astronomer.

- **Fashion:** Silk and other new fabrics were used to design and make fashionable clothes for rich people.

- **Art:** Artists such as Holbein, van Dyck and Lely came from Germany and the Netherlands to paint royalty and other rich people. Their paintings were admired and gradually merchants and bankers wanted their portraits painted as well.

- **Writing:** Polydore Vergil was born in Italy and migrated to England, spending most of his life in London. He was one of the first people to write a book about English history.

The printing press

The invention of the printing press took control of knowledge away from the Church and enabled new ideas to spread. By 1535, about two-thirds of those working in the book trade in England were European.

Now try this

Choose **two** ways in which Huguenots made an impact on England. For each way, say why it was important.

Sandwich and Canterbury

Case study Flemish and Walloon migrants were Protestants who, in the 16th century, fled Catholic persecution in what is now Belgium and the Netherlands. Although these migrants had similar skills, their experiences were very different as they contributed to the local economy in Kent.

Flemish weavers in Sandwich

1561 Officials in the town of Sandwich, worried about the town's declining prosperity, got permission from Elizabeth I's Council to invite Flemish weavers to Sandwich. They were to work only in the weaving or fishing industries.

1561 Flemish weavers began to arrive in Sandwich. They wove high-quality woollen broadcloth that sold well in the twice-weekly town markets. They were given St Peter's church so they could worship in their own way.

1569 English people in Sandwich began to complain that the Flemish were taking 'their jobs'. In 1569 Sandwich officials ruled that migrants could only work in trades other than weaving and fishing if no Englishman could be found to do the work. Migrants would be fined if they disobeyed the ruling. Some migrants were so successful that they set up different businesses – for example in tailoring or farming – but were fined for doing so.

1582 There were over 1,500 Flemish weavers in Sandwich by 1582, almost half of the town's population. They appealed to Elizabeth I's Council, saying the Sandwich officials were being unfair. The Council repeated the ruling that the Flemish migrants were only to work in weaving and fishing while they were living in Sandwich, but gave them permission to move and work elsewhere.

Hundreds of Flemish migrants moved to live and work in other English towns and cities.

Walloon weavers in Canterbury

Canterbury, like Sandwich, was in decline. In 1575 Elizabeth I's Council gave the city permission to invite Walloon migrants from Europe and elsewhere in England to live and work there.

The city authorities gave 100 empty houses to the Walloons as well as a disused monastery. The Walloons converted the monastery buildings into a church, a school, a weavers' hall and a market. It became the centre of the Walloon community.

The Walloons had twelve 'elders' who set rules and kept order in the community. They worked closely with the local authorities.

Weavers at work. Some Walloons had been working in Sandwich. In 1575 they were invited by city officials to move to Canterbury.

The Walloon weavers were very successful as they produced high-quality cloth. By 1600 over 3,000 Walloons were living and working in Canterbury, almost one-third of its population.

Many became rich and built their own houses and workshops. They employed English people living there and passed on their skills.

Walloons developed new trades, like silk dying and diamond cutting, that didn't previously exist in the city. Trade in the area improved greatly and Canterbury prospered.

Now try this

State **one** difference and **one** similarity between the experiences of the Flemish migrants in Sandwich and the Walloon migrants in Canterbury.

The experience of the Huguenots

Case study In the period 1670 to 1710 between 40,000 and 50,000 Huguenots fled to England. At least half of them settled in London – a few in Soho but most in Spitalfields. Spitalfields became known as 'weaver town'.

Living and working in Spitalfields

There was already a small silk-weaving industry in Spitalfields, but the arrival of thousands of Huguenot families, some with money to invest, changed the area completely. The new arrivals were often welcomed by relatives already settled in England.

Large numbers of workshops were built that employed hundreds of weavers and made their owners, the master weavers and merchants, extremely wealthy.

Many Huguenots in Spitalfields were skilled businessmen too, and some made an enormous amount of money. Between 1650 and 1700, England's production of silk fabrics increased 20 times, largely due to Spitalfields' weavers.

Huguenot weavers sometimes used their houses as workshops, so they had large windows to maximise light.

The first Huguenot migrants settled in Spitalfields because housing was cheap. As they prospered, master weavers built new houses or adapted old ones.

Huguenots in Spitalfields were highly skilled silk weavers who wove a variety of different fabrics in silk, some of which were beautifully patterned. Spitalfields was outside the City of London and so the weavers were free from the rules of the guilds and could experiment with the sorts of cloth they wove.

Weavers' guilds were organisations that laid down rules about the quality and type of cloth that could be woven.

Huguenot churches in Spitalfields

Huguenots were able to keep their own cultural identity such as language, clothes and food. Their religion was an important part of this.

- The Huguenots asked the authorities for permission to build their own churches. By 1700, nine had been built.

- Links between the churches meant that Huguenots knew about other immigrants, including new arrivals, so they could help anyone who had fallen on hard times.

- Huguenots were more readily accepted into English society than some other migrants. This was because they were seen as having Protestant values: church-going, respectable and hardworking. This helped English people to develop a more tolerant attitude towards migrants.

Support from monarchs

Charles II offered Huguenots 'denizen status'. This and the Foreign Protestants Nationality Act (1708) gave Huguenots in England more security.

William III and Mary II were Protestants. They became joint monarchs in 1689 and took a special interest in the Huguenots.

- In 1689 William issued a Declaration stating that he would 'support, aid and assist' Huguenots to make their lives 'comfortable and easy'.

- One result of the Declaration was to set up a relief committee to help the Huguenots settle in. By 1700 over £64,000 had been raised.

- Between 1689 and 1693, William and Mary donated £39,000 to help Huguenot settlement in London.

Riots threatened to break out in Spitalfields in 1675, 1681 and 1683 when English weavers complained that Huguenots were taking away their jobs. These disturbances quickly ended when the Huguenots offered to teach their skills to the English weavers.

Now try this

List at least **three** reasons why the Huguenots prospered in Spitalfields in the 17th century. Then decide which you think was the most important reason and explain why.

18th- and 19th-century Britain

Britain was the first country in the world to have an industrial revolution. This was a huge change for British society. It had a tremendous impact on people moving within Britain as well as people migrating to Britain.

Towns and cities like Bradford and Manchester grew rapidly. This is called urbanisation. The number of people living in towns grew from under 5 million in 1700 to approximately 32.5 million in 1900. This was because of the rapid growth of work available in factories as a result of industrialisation.

Transport links involving roads, canals and railways were improved. It became easier and quicker to take raw materials to factories and finished goods to the docks. The new docks in Liverpool, London, Glasgow, Hull and Bristol, for example, were the busiest in the world as trade links grew and developed.

The impact of the industrial revolution

Agriculture changed: enclosure of fields meant that better crops were grown and high-quality meat and wool were produced. This met the needs of the growing towns for more food, even though fewer people were needed to work the land.

Demands from the growing towns and cities led to wider representation in Parliament as middle-class and, by the end of the century, working-class men were able to vote – and vote in secrecy. Laws passed by Parliament showed a gradual change in attitudes to, for example, the transatlantic slave trade and slavery. People felt freer to express different attitudes to the ways in which society should be run and to demand their civil liberties (their rights to, for example, free speech).

The British Empire

In the 17th century England gained its first colonies. They were on the east coast of North America as well as some islands in the Caribbean. In the period 1700–1900 this developed into the vast British Empire.

Timeline

1783 American colonies became independent from Britain and its empire and formed the United States of America.

1840 New Zealand became a British colony.

1881 onwards Britain gained colonies in Africa stretching from Cairo to Cape Town.

1763 Canada became a British colony.

1788 Australia became a British colony.

1858 The British government took control of India.

1900 Britain ruled one-fifth of the world's land and a quarter of the world's population by this date.

The transatlantic slave trade

By 1750 Britain sold more black Africans into slavery in the Caribbean than any other European nation. This was part of the British Triangular Trade:

* 3.5 million black Africans were transported across the Atlantic in British ships. They were sold into slavery on sugar and cotton plantations in the Caribbean and the southern states of America

* The ships returned to Britain with cargoes of sugar, cotton, tobacco and rum.

* As enslaved people laboured in brutal conditions, slave traders became very rich. They reinvested their profits from trading humans back in Britain, often in buildings such as town halls and schools.

Britain used its empire as a source of raw materials and a market for its manufactured goods. This often destroyed local industries, for example the Indian cotton industry.

Now try this

Write a paragraph describing at least **three** ways in which the changes resulting from the British Industrial Revolution would attract migrants.

Migration and settlement

There were both change and continuity behind the reasons for migration to Britain in the 18th and 19th centuries. Some people were forced to migrate while others made a deliberate choice to do so. All believed they would lead better lives in Britain.

Irish migrants

The whole of Ireland was part of Britain at this time. It was mainly rural, and a lot of the land was poor quality. It was usual for Irish people to cross to England or Scotland to work for a few weeks where they could earn more money than in Ireland. Then they would go back home. In the 1840s and 1850s however, it was different because Ireland was hit by a terrible famine.

- Tens of thousands of Irish people migrated to England and Scotland. They were fleeing poverty and starvation in search of a better life. Many believed their chances of survival were better in mainland Britain than in Ireland.

- Liverpool and Glasgow were the nearest ports to Belfast and Dublin so were quicker and cheaper to reach. Many Irish migrants settled in these cities.

- Many migrants regarded Britain as a 'stop-over' on their way to America or Australia. However, hundreds found they couldn't afford the fare to travel further, so they stayed in Britain. They usually lived in the poorest parts of cities, often in Irish communities that were already there.

Rural occupations such as spinning and weaving had collapsed in Ireland because of English competition. English factories produced the same goods more quickly and at lower cost.

Migrants from the British Empire and beyond

The expansion of Britain's empire and new trading routes meant that many different people migrated to Britain.

- When English families returned to Britain from India, their Indian servants often chose to go with them to keep their jobs. Usually this would be the family's ayah but sometimes men servants too.

- Indian students migrated to study at British universities. Many studied Law.

  See page 8 for information on ayahs.

- Some Indian princes came to Britain as they preferred the way Britain was ruled.

- The East India Company recruited sailors (lascars) from India, China, Malaya, Somalia and Yemen to transport their goods to Britain. The working conditions on ships were poor so many lascars stayed in British ports in search of a better life. Others were abandoned by their employers.

The East India Company

The Company was formed in 1600 to trade in the Indian Ocean. Eventually it ran vast areas of India, with its own army and administrators. From 1858 the British government ruled India in what was called the British Raj.

Migrants from Europe and the Russian Empire

Jews	Italians	Germans
• They came to join existing Jewish communities in Britain. • Although anti-Semitism still existed, there was increasing tolerance in Britain, especially compared with the persecution Jews faced in the Russian Empire.	• Agriculture in Britain was prosperous compared to that in Italy. • Britain was peaceful and less dangerous than Italy, which was at war and had outbreaks of typhus and cholera.	• Britain had greater freedom for political thinkers to express their ideas and greater opportunities – it was free from government interference for skilled people. • Britain was peaceful compared with the warfare between German states.

Now try this

Make a table of differences between the reasons why people migrated to Britain from Ireland and India in the period c1700–c1900.

Had a look ☐   Nearly there ☐   Nailed it! ☐

Migrants: Experience

In the period c1700–c1900, most migrants lived in Britain's crowded towns and cities. Dirt, disease and early death were common, but the Industrial Revolution provided many job opportunities.

Migrant experiences in industrial Britain

Irish migrants
- Most Irish migrants settled in Britain's industrialising cities and took on labouring work as few had the skills needed for factory work.
- Irish navvies (labourers) dug canals and constructed railways. The work was hard, dirty and dangerous. Many navvies were killed while they were at work, pushing their families into poverty.
- Irish migrants faced prejudice from many English people because they were Catholics living in a Protestant country and worked for lower wages than the English.
- Some English people also thought that all Irish migrants were Fenians – Irish independence fighters – who ran bombing campaigns in London and other cities in the 1880s.

European migrants
- German migrants settled throughout Britain, but Italians settled mainly in London.
- Some German engineers and scientists set up companies that became very successful. For example, the Brunner-Mond company in Liverpool.
- Hundreds of Germans set up small businesses such as shops and restaurants.
- Some Italians continued working as they had done in Italy, making tiles and ceramics or labouring on the roads. Other Italians developed new skills, such as making and selling ice cream and working as street musicians.
- Because they contributed to the economy, German and Italian migrants were generally well regarded.

The Suez canal opened in 1869. It made the journey between India and Britain much quicker and so increased the opportunities for Asian people to migrate to Britain.

Jewish migrants
- New Jewish migrants settled in established Jewish communities, where they were supported until they found work.
- Many of the new migrant Jews worked in the clothing industry.
- New Jewish migrants faced anti-Semitism. They were seen as being different in their clothes, food, language and religion.
- Many English people thought their income was threatened because new Jewish migrants were often prepared to work longer hours for lower wages. The authorities could do nothing to stop this and the unions were furious because they had fought long and hard to get hours of work regulated.

Some settled Jews were afraid that the arrival of thousands of poor Jewish families would cause an increase in anti-Semitism. They worried that they would lose their existing carefully won acceptance. They were wary of helping newcomers.

Asian migrants: ayahs and lascars
- Many ayahs stayed with their families when those families moved to England and later they found work with other English families.
- Some ayahs were abandoned by their English employers and became destitute. A Christian charity set up a hostel for them and either raised money for their passage back to India or found them work in England.
- Some lascars were abandoned by their shipping companies when they reached port, but others chose to leave their ships.
- Many lascars found work in the ports. Others became destitute, begging and stealing to keep alive. Hostels were set up to help them.

The role of the media

The media played an important part in changing social attitudes toward migrants.

- Newspapers publicised the judgement of Lord Justice Mansfield (1772) when he said that slavery did not legally exist in England. This judgement delighted many black Africans in Britain as well as those who wanted slavery and the transatlantic slave trade to end. Those who benefited from the trade were less happy.
- Paul Reuter, a German migrant, started the London-based Reuters News Agency in 1851. It sold international news to British newspapers and made British readers feel part of a wider world.
- Newspapers publicised the plight of Mary Seacole, a Jamaican nurse who was left destitute after caring for soldiers during the Crimean War. A fund-raising gala was held in 1858 which raised a substantial amount of money due to publicity she received.

The rail network carried newspapers all over Britain, so what they printed was widely read.

Now try this

Describe the main problem faced by many Asian migrants in Britain in the period c1700–c1900.

Migrants: Impact

Migrants from Africa, Asia and Europe had a tremendous impact in Britain in the 18th and 19th centuries. They brought change to many different aspects of British society, including culture, trade and industry, politics and the urban environment.

Politics and parliament

- Black Africans, some of whom had been enslaved, for example Olaudah Equiano, helped persuade the public and MPs that the transatlantic slave trade and slavery itself, should be abolished. In 1807 Parliament voted to abolish the transatlantic slave trade, and in 1833 to abolish slavery in the British Empire.

- The ideas of German migrants Karl Marx and Friedrich Engels had a significant impact on the way people believed society should be organised. Their *Communist Manifesto* outlined how industry and property should be owned and run by the community – they believed this would make society fairer.

- Some migrants became involved with Chartism, a national movement that wanted working-class representation in Parliament. Feargus O'Connor, an Irish Protestant, edited the *Northern Star*, a radical newspaper that supported the Chartists. William Cuffay, whose father had been enslaved in the Caribbean, became chairman of the London Chartists.

After buying his freedom from slavery, Olaudah Equiano settled in Britain and became a well-known anti-slavery campaigner.

Jews gained more civil rights throughout this period. Lionel de Rothschild became the first Jewish MP in 1858.

In 1829 Parliament passed the Catholic Emancipation Act that gave Catholics almost all the same civil rights as everyone else. However, they still couldn't attend universities, hold certain public offices or become monarch.

Trade and industry

- Irish navvies, by digging canals and constructing railways, played a huge part in making Britain's economy successful. By the 1880s, a rail network linked all the major cities, towns and ports, transporting raw materials and finished goods.

- Migrants owned and ran shops, banks and businesses. Many did very well and helped the British economy grow and prosper. For example, in 1884 Michael Marks, a Polish Jew, owned a stall in Leeds market. By 1900 Marks & Spencer had shops in all Britain's major towns.

- Many migrants were employed in and helped some industries thrive. For example, many Eastern European Jews worked in the clothing trade.

The urban environment

Migrants and their work changed the appearance of towns and cities. For example:

- Railways went into town and city centres.

- Synagogues were built so Jews could worship in line with their own beliefs. By 1900 a small number of mosques had also been built for Muslims to worship.

Culture

Migrants' culture had an impact beyond their own communities.

- Chinese, Indian and Jewish restaurants and cafes added variety to people's diets.

- The music of Samuel Coleridge-Taylor, the son of a black African father and his English wife, was enjoyed by many and helped to break down racial prejudice.

Now try this

Create a simple concept map on the impact of Irish migrants on Britain c1700–c1900.

Liverpool

Case study Liverpool had prospered from the transatlantic slave trade. Traders, who had made fortunes from plantations worked by enslaved people in terrible conditions, invested in the city. The transatlantic slave trade ended in England in 1807 and slavery ended in the British Empire in 1833. Merchants began importing and exporting a wide range of goods instead. In the 19th century Liverpool became a flourishing port with migrant communities living there.

The growth of the port of Liverpool

Liverpool faced the Atlantic Ocean and so Liverpool merchants traded mainly with America, importing raw materials and exporting finished goods.

Raw cotton was Liverpool's main import. It was needed to meet the demands of the growing number of spinning and weaving mills in nearby Manchester. About 80% of Britain's cotton imports came from the USA, mostly through the port of Liverpool.

The port of Liverpool in the 19th century.

In 1845, Liverpool's docks handled 2.5 million tons of goods. By 1900, the port had 7 miles of docks that handled 10.5 million tons of goods. Liverpool was the second most profitable port in the world, second only to London.

Steamships gradually replaced sailing ships. They were faster, could carry more cargo and needed less skill to sail.

Liverpool was very attractive to migrants as work seemed to be readily available.

The Irish community

- Irish navvies built the docks and thousands of migrants worked on them afterwards as dockers and warehousemen.

- After the 1840s Irish businesses opened. Irish pubs gave advice and support to new arrivals.

- By 1851, over 20% of the population of the city was Irish (83,000 people). Most of them lived in poor, run-down districts of the city – areas where disease flourished.

- Irish people who fell ill were looked after by the Liverpool Workhouse Infirmary. In 1847, 60,000 caught typhus, a disease associated with filthy living conditions. Huge sheds by the docks were used to isolate those with the disease and restrictions were put on Irish migrants coming in to Liverpool. The disease was known as 'Irish fever' and caused a lot of resentment among the English population.

- Most Irish migrants were Catholics. In 1870 there were 8 Catholic parishes in the city. By 1916, there were 24.

Sailors

Many lascars stayed on in Liverpool once their ships had docked.

Indian sailors
Some carried on working as sailors for other shipping lines; others took what work they could find; and some set up lodging houses. Many married English women, which helped them settle in the community. In 1890 a mosque was opened for Muslim Indians.

Chinese sailors
From the 1850s, Liverpool merchants began trading in silk and tea from Shanghai and Hong Kong. Chinese sailors stayed on in Liverpool, setting up businesses, shops and cafes. They gained a reputation for hard work. Soon, Liverpool had the largest Chinatown in Europe. Many married English women. They became well known for the support they gave their families.

African sailors
Increasing trade with Africa brought African sailors to Liverpool. Many were hired by shipping companies because they were willing to work for lower wages and in worse conditions than other sailors.

Many people were prejudiced against the Irish migrants and crime was often blamed on them. In 1850 half of the 6,000 people brought before the magistrates were Irish.

Now try this

Give **two** advantages and **two** disadvantages of being an Irish migrant in Liverpool in the period c1700 to c1900.

Jewish migrants in London

 Case study In the late 19th century, a large number of Jewish migrants from Eastern Europe and Russia arrived in Britain. Facing persecution at home, they saw Britain as a safe place.

Living and working in the East End of London

In the years after 1880, about 150,000 Jews arrived in London. Many had been travelling for weeks, desperate to reach the safety of Britain, and were very weary. Their journeys had been long and uncomfortable. They had brought with them only what they could carry: a suitcase containing their belongings, bedding, crockery, some tools of their trade and little money.

Whitechapel and Spitalfields were areas in the East End of London, where most of the new Jewish migrants headed. Here there were established Jewish communities – but living and working conditions were poor.

An engraving of Wentworth Street, Whitechapel, where many migrant Jews lived.

Jewish community leaders established a 'shelter' where migrants could stay for a maximum of 14 days. They were given two meals a day while they found other accommodation and work.

Many Jewish people found work in sweatshops, where they worked long hours in poor conditions for little pay. They produced a range of clothing from cheap to expensive.

The new migrants spoke little if any English. Jewish leaders introduced a crash course in the English language and customs. This would help the new migrants integrate yet allow them to retain their Jewish heritage.

The Jewish Free School was important in educating London's Jewish children in their new way of life.

Sweatshops

There was unemployment in the East End and the arrival of thousands of Jews looking for work created a tense situation.

- Many English people living in London believed that Jews working in sweatshops were taking work away from them.

- Trade unions had worked hard to establish basic working conditions, However, sweatshop owners ignored them and produced goods more cheaply than properly regulated factories.

- All sweatshops were illegal, wherever they were run in England. Not all sweatshops were owned by Jews but the ones in Whitechapel were. This made it particularly difficult to shut them down. This was because the owners only spoke Yiddish (a language spoken by Jewish people in many parts of the world), which the police did not. So there was a communication problem.

Racial tension

There was so much violence targeting Jewish people that the police were afraid to patrol the streets alone in some areas. Parliament set up two committees of enquiry into anti-Semitism.

When five women were murdered by a man nicknamed 'Jack the Ripper', some blamed the Jewish community:

- There was a suggestion that the knives of Jewish ritual slaughterers had been used, but this was not true.

- Graffiti blaming Jewish people was found near the bloodstained apron belonging to one of the victims, but the connection to the murder could not be proved.

- Various witnesses testified that they had seen the women talking to 'foreigners' before they were killed, but this was not verified.

The murderer was never caught and anti-Semitism continued to increase.

Now try this

Write a paragraph explaining how sweatshops increased anti-Semitism in the East End of London.

Modern Britain

There were many changes in British society in the years from 1900. These changes led to many opportunities for migration to Britain that various governments tried to control.

The First World War, 1914–18	The Second World War, 1939–45
• Over 3 million men from the British Empire, including 1 million from India, served on the Allies' side, mainly on the Western Front. • Thousands of lascars worked on merchant navy ships, especially on Atlantic convoys, bringing food and supplies to Britain. This released men to join the Royal Navy. • The British economy was wholly prepared for war production.	• About 8 million men from the British Empire, including 2.5 million from India, served on the Allies' side. Most fought in the Far East and Africa. • Thousands of migrant seamen worked on merchant ships bringing food to Britain. • Cities and ports, factories and houses, as well as road and rail links throughout Britain, were all bombed, damaged and destroyed.

Empire, Commonwealth and the EU

End of Empire
In the years 1700 to 1900, the British Empire had been strong. But after 1945, it became clear that Britain could not retain large parts of its empire.
• Britain's economy was shattered. It could not afford to spend money on maintaining an empire. Decolonisation had to begin.
• Many colonies had been developing their own independence movements. India gained independence in 1947 and was followed by many other countries in the 1950s and 1960s.

The Commonwealth
In 1949, the Commonwealth of Nations was formed. Membership meant countries that had gained independence could keep links with Britain and each other.

The European Union (EU)
In 1973, Britain joined the European Economic Community (EEC). It had 9 members; by 2007 there were 23 members and the EEC had become the EU. In 2016, the British people voted to leave the EU.

Most of Ireland became independent in 1922, leaving only the six north-eastern counties (Northern Ireland) as part of the UK.

Key term
 Decolonisation is when one country stops governing others and the former colonies become independent countries.

Legislation

As the 20th century progressed, some English people felt that too many migrants were arriving. In response, Parliament passed legislation on immigration and nationality. This limited the number of people who could enter the country.

1905 Aliens Act: Only people with jobs or money could migrate to Britain.

1948 British Nationality Act: Millions of people in the British colonies and former colonies were given the right to enter Britain and stay.

1962 Commonwealth Immigrants Act: A voucher system was introduced. Only those with a valuable skill or who could get a job where there was a shortage of workers were able to get a voucher and so permission to migrate.

1968 Commonwealth Immigrants Act: The number of vouchers available was reduced. Applicants had to have been born in Britain or have parents or grandparents born there.

1971 Immigration Act: Vouchers were replaced with work permits for specific time periods. These didn't apply to people with British-born parents or grandparents.

1981 Nationality Act: The automatic right to stay in Britain was no longer possible for non-British citizens.

Now try this

Imagine you are a migrant who came to Britain in the years 1945 to 1950. Write a brief letter to a relative giving at least **one** reason why you chose to migrate to Britain in this period.

Migration and settlement

There are many reasons why so many people migrated to and settled in Britain after 1900.

Seeking safety from war: During the First World War 250,000 Belgians fled to Britain, as did 160,000 Polish people during the Second World War. They regarded Britain as a place of safety. The 1905 Aliens Act was suspended to allow them into the country. Most Belgians returned to Belgium in 1919, but many Poles decided to remain after 1945 because Poland had become a communist state. There is, for example, a large Polish community in Bradford, West Yorkshire.

Encouragement to migrate: There weren't enough migrants coming from Europe to help rebuild. Therefore, the government started to encourage people from the colonies, particularly from the Caribbean, to migrate to Britain. As well as for rebuilding, this was also for working on the buses and trains in the London Transport system and working in the National Health Service (NHS), launched in 1948. The third ship to bring migrants from the Caribbean is the best known, the Empire Windrush. It docked at Tilbury in June 1948 with over 800 migrants.

The world wars

Looking for work: Following the Second World War, there was plenty of employment available in Britain, rebuilding everything that bombing had destroyed. People from all over Europe travelled to work in Britain's bombed cities.

Seeking safety from persecution: Between December 1938 and September 1939, over 8,000 Jewish children travelled to safety in Britain on their own. The children were escaping Nazi persecution and the rescue mission was called 'Kindertransport'. They were due to return home after the war, but most of their relatives perished in the Holocaust.

The Empire and Commonwealth

Many migrated from Britain's former colonies. They sought a better quality of life, free from war and persecution.

India and Pakistan 1947: Independence caused terrible violence when the country was partitioned into India and Pakistan. Thousands migrated to Britain.

⬇

Kenya 1967: Kenya had a large Asian population. Four years after independence, President Jomo Kenyatta asked all Asians in Kenya to choose between being Kenyan and being British – 95,000 chose to remain British. All non-Kenyans could only remain on a temporary basis. By 1968, 20,000 had migrated to Britain and settled, mainly in London and Leicester.

⬇

Uganda 1972: As in Kenya, the Asian community in Uganda played a large part in creating the country's prosperity. Idi Amin first ordered their expulsion, but then insisted the professionals had to stay. After failed negotiations, the British government offered Asians in Uganda either an Indian or a British passport if they wanted to leave: 27,000 chose to go to Britain. Thousands settled in Leicester.

Other reasons for migration

The EU
Britain's membership of the EU gave EU citizens the right to enter Britain. After 2004, nine Eastern European states joined. Thousands migrated to Britain to find work that was better paid than in their own country.

Ireland
After 1900 migration from Ireland continued at comparatively high levels. Irish citizens were exempt from the 1905 Aliens Act and were allowed to migrate to Britain after the Republic of Ireland became independent in 1922. Most came for the work opportunities in Britain and to join family and existing Irish communities.

Asylum seekers and refugees
In 1951 Britain signed the United Nations Convention on Refugees, agreeing to offer asylum to people facing persecution. Migrants came to Britain to avoid dangerous situations in their home countries.

Many migrants applied for asylum and arrived in Britain legally. However, desperate refugees sometimes resorted to paying smugglers to enter Britain illegally.

Look back to page 7 to remind yourself about the Huguenots.

Now try this

The Huguenots migrated to England in the 16th century and people from the Caribbean in the 20th century. Find **one** similarity and **one** difference in the reasons why these groups migrated.

Migrants: Experience

Migrants who have arrived in Britain since 1900 have had very mixed experiences. Difficulties have often been linked to poor living conditions and unemployment.

Suspicion and support before 1945	Suspicion and hostility after 1945

• In 1914–18 Belgians were welcomed. Many set up small businesses. About 90% returned to Belgium.
• In 1914 Germans in Britain were declared 'enemy aliens' and were interned (put in prison for political reasons). People attacked German shops and businesses.
• In 1918 sailors who had joined the Royal Navy couldn't return to their old jobs on merchant ships. The shipping companies continued to employ lascars who would work for less money. There were riots in the docks.
• In 1936 the British Union of Fascists (BUF) held a march through an area of London with a large Jewish population. Fighting broke out in Cable Street between the marchers, supporters of the Jewish community and the police who were trying to force the march through. In the end the police diverted the march elsewhere. This became known as the Battle of Cable Street.
• In 1939 Jewish children arriving via *Kindertransport* were welcomed.
• Between 1939 and 1945 most Germans living and working in Britain were not interned; many had fled to the safety of Britain from Nazi Germany.
• In 1940 the BUF was disbanded when Britain was at war with Germany.
	• In 1947 the Polish Resettlement Act gave Poles the right to remain. Polish communities grew in many towns and cities and gained wide acceptance.
	• In 1967 the National Front (NF) was founded to oppose immigration. Members believed that only white people should be British citizens.
	• In 1968 politician Enoch Powell made what was later called the 'rivers of blood' speech. He criticised immigration, especially from the Commonwealth and called for immigrants to be 'sent back'.
	• In 1982 the British National Party (BNP) was founded. Members opposed non-white migration to Britain.
	• In some cities, racial tension reached breaking point and people fought in the streets. For example:
	  – 1981, Brixton, London: Riots, which lasted for 3 days, were triggered by accusations of police brutality against migrants.
	  – 2001, Burnley, Lancashire: A weekend of rioting was triggered by a dispute between Asian and white drug gangs.

Race relations legislation

The aim of this legislation was to encourage better relationships between communities. It was closely linked to the legislation that limited immigration. Governments wanted immigrants to integrate into British society and believed that could only be done if immigration was limited.

The Brixton riots 1981. All riots were widely reported and discussed in the media.

Timeline

1968 Race Relations Act: Discrimination in housing and employment were made illegal.

1998 Crime and Disorder Act: It introduced more severe punishments if a crime was seen to have been aggravated by racism.

1965 Race Relations Act: This was the first Act to make some types of racial discrimination illegal.

1976 Race Relations Act: This set up a Commission for Racial Equality to use the law to prevent racial discrimination and raise public awareness of racial injustice.

Newspapers, television and, later, the Internet all had a huge impact on people's opinions. Some parts of the media portrayed migrants negatively, which stirred up prejudice against immigrants. Others portrayed migrants more positively. Some campaigned against racism.

Many migrants and some white English people campaigned for more equal rights for non-white people. This helped persuade Parliament to pass race relations legislation.

Now try this

Write a summary of the anti-immigration movement of post-1900 Britain.

Migrants: Impact

In modern Britain, migrants have played a vital part in the British economy and society. This is particularly true for the years immediately after the Second World War.

In this period, as in earlier ones, migrants faced prejudice from the existing population. Many were forced to work below the level for which they were qualified, though sometimes this could be because qualifications from other countries differed.

Transport, public services and industry

- Migrants, particularly those from the Caribbean, played a vital part in building up Britain's transport systems after the Second World War. For example, in 1968 London Transport employed 73,000 people, including 9,000 from the Caribbean. London Transport employed women as well as men from the Caribbean as bus conductors, station staff and canteen workers and, later, as bus drivers.
- Migrants, for example, Irish and Italian migrants, played a major role in rebuilding Britain's industry after the Second World War. For example, by 1971, nearly 300,000 migrants worked in manufacturing and engineering, mainly in the West Midlands.
- Migrants were urgently needed to work as doctors and nurses, cleaners and porters. Many came from Eastern Europe, India and Pakistan. They were vital at the start of the NHS and in keeping it running. About 12% of doctors in 1953–55 had been trained overseas. In 2003, 29.4% of NHS doctors and 43.5% of NHS nurses were born overseas.

A migrant worker in Britain.

The impact of migrants in Britain

Politics

- **Harold Moody** founded the League of Coloured Peoples in 1931. It campaigned for civil rights and helped many black people deal with the prejudice they faced.
- **Doreen Lawrence** claimed the police had been incompetent and racist in failing to find her son Stephen Lawrence's murderer. In 1999, six years after Stephen's murder, a public enquiry found that the Metropolitan Police were institutionally racist.
- **Show Racism the Red Card** is a charity working to stamp out racism in football. Started in Tyneside in 1996 it has spread throughout Britain.
- The **Black Lives Matter** movement protests against racially motivated violence. It began in the USA in 2013 and spread worldwide after the murder of George Floyd in May 2020. In June 2020, protest marches were held across the UK. The Internet has had a tremendous impact on the spread of the movement.

Culture and the urban environment

- Migrants renovated areas where they lived.
- They often ran small corner shops that opened from early to late and served the whole community.
- Migrants' communities became lively places to visit, especially during festivals or religious celebrations like Diwali, Eid al-Fitr and the Chinese New Year.
- The urban environment was changed by buildings such as mosques and synagogues. Colourful entrances to migrant communities, like that to Chinatown, Manchester, attracted visitors.
- Migrants introduced new foods such as pizzas, sausages, kebabs, Chow Mein and Chicken Tikka Masala. This changed the British diet.
- Migrants and their descendants have made an impact on different aspects of British life, such as politics, music, broadcasting and sport. For example, Diane Abbott, the first black woman to be elected to Parliament; Mo Farah, winner of several Olympic gold medals; and Trevor McDonald, TV broadcaster.

The 'Windrush generation' of migrants were badly treated, later, by immigration officials who denied their right to stay in Britain. This was despite the fact that they had been living in Britain for many years. After media coverage and public uproar, the government apologised and offered compensation.

Leaving the EU

The number of migrants coming to Britain, mostly from EU countries, rose in the 21st century. In 2016, Britain voted to leave the EU. Many gave immigration as their main reason for voting to leave.

Now try this

Choose **one** area of focus: transport, **or** the NHS **or** industry. Describe **one** impact migrants made on this area and say why this was important to the British economy.

Bristol

Case study After 1948 Caribbean migrants arrived to help rebuild war-damaged Bristol. By 1958 there were 1,500 migrants in the city and by 1962, there were 3,000. Living and working there, migrants made an impact on the city, despite facing prejudice and racism.

Many landlords refused to rent to black people. They were forced to live in bomb-damaged areas of the city, such as St Paul's, where many families shared one house.

By the 1960s, many Caribbean residents lived within a few streets of each other. Many believed it was safer to live close together in case of trouble.

Experiencing problems and prejudice

Some white people believed that Caribbean migrants were taking their jobs. This heightened tensions especially when there was a rise in unemployment.

The Bristol Bus Boycott, 1963

In 1955 the Transport and General Workers Union banned black and Asian people from being hired as bus drivers or conductors in the UK. The Bristol Omnibus Company agreed. The ban stayed in place for several years.

In November 1962 a group of migrants set up the West Indian Development Council (WIDC). Its aim was to combat racism and to advise Caribbean migrants on matters concerning education, housing and employment.

Colour bar means refusing goods or services to people because of the colour of their skin.

Early in 1963 the WIDC decided to challenge the colour bar on the buses. They asked Guy Bailey to apply for a job with the Bristol Omnibus Company. His offer of an interview was withdrawn as soon as the company was told he was a Caribbean migrant.

On 29 April 1963, the WIDC called on the black community to boycott Bristol's buses. They did. Many white people joined in. A march took place on 6 May 1963 and the boycott got national attention.

On 28 August 1963, the company gave in to public pressure and scrapped the ban. In September they employed an Indian bus conductor. Progress was slow. A year after the 1965 Race Relations Act, over 97.5% of Bristol's bus drivers and conductors were white.

In 1975 the WIDC changed its name to The West Indian Parents and Friends Association and continued to fight racism and support the black community.

Culture: St Paul's Carnival

The first carnival held in St Paul's in 1968 started as a festival. It brought together St Paul's residents and local activists. It was a relatively small affair, where people opened their homes and their gardens, played music and ate street food.

Held every year, it is now a one-day carnival celebrating African–Caribbean culture. People from different communities take part and watch, helping to develop an understanding of the richness of different cultures.

The role of individuals

Roy Hackett, born in Jamaica, helped found the WIDC, organise the Bristol Bus Boycott and the St Paul's Festivals.

Princess Campbell, born in Jamaica, trained as a nurse and became Bristol's first black ward sister. She set up the United Housing Association to help black people find affordable housing.

Barbara Dettering, born in British Guyana, was a teacher and social worker in St Paul's for 18 years and supported the WIDC.

Now try this

Describe **two** ways in which Caribbean migrants in Bristol helped to reduce racism in the mid-20th century.

Asian migrants in Leicester

 Case study From 1945 Asian migrants in Leicester were generally very successful in business and brought prosperity to the city. However, their experience was not always positive.

Migration to Leicester

In 1951 there were 624 Asians living in Leicester. By 1981 this had risen to 59,709. Asian migrants came to Leicester because:

- There was plenty of housing and work available, particularly in the textile and shoe industries.
- Many Asian people found help and support in Leicester. The British Asian Welfare Society helped the new arrivals find jobs and homes.
- Asians could easily follow their own religion. By 1972 Leicester had three Hindu temples, three Sikh gurdwaras and two mosques. Social and welfare clubs were well-established: there were 40 by 1972.

Migrants arrived from India, Pakistan and Bangladesh. They sought safety and stability during the civil war that followed the partition of India in 1947. Thousands more Asians arrived from Kenya from 1967 and Uganda from 1972.

See page 19 for information on what happened to Asians in Kenya and Uganda.

Discouragement and racism

The city council generally welcomed Asian migrants, though there were worries about numbers. Not everyone was as welcoming.

In the early years of Asian migration, the local press was concerned about multiculturalism, preferring the Asian community to remain separate. Later, the local press were full of praise for the Asian community and their hard work in bringing prosperity to Leicester.

- In August 1972 the city council told the Home Office that the city was 'full up'. The council ran a series of advertisements in the Ugandan press discouraging Asians from going to Leicester.
- The National Front targeted Leicester. In 1974 and 1979 they organised marches there to protest against immigration.

See page 20 for information on the National Front.

- Trade unions worried that jobs would go to Asians instead of white British people. Many Asians had to take work for which they were overqualified. They were generally paid less than white workers doing the same job.

The impact of Asian migrants on the city of Leicester

In 1967 the Race Equality Centre was founded, based on the Commission for Racial Equality. It helped thousands of migrants from Asia, Africa and the Caribbean.

Many Asian migrants had been successful business-owners in Uganda and they brought that experience and expertise with them. By 1994 there were 1,446 Asian-owned businesses in Leicester. Ten years later, there were over 10,000 British Asian-owned businesses in Leicester – they employed thousands of people and contributed greatly to the British economy.

Celebrating Diwali in Leicester's Golden Mile.

In the 1970s, Asian immigrants took over empty shops in Belgrave Road, selling clothing and food. Now, called 'the Golden Mile', because of the number of jewellers' shops, it is a thriving shopping area and tourist attraction.

Two major festivals are held every year in Leicester. Since 1982, the Mela Festival has been a celebration of South Asian Arts and Indian culture. Diwali, the Festival of Light, is held every November lasting for five days and is celebrated by Hindus, Sikhs and Jains.

Now try this

Write a brief summary of the experience of Asian migrants in Leicester since 1945.

Britain after 1945

After the Second World War, Britain faced many national and regional challenges. However, by the 1960s (the 'Swinging Sixties'), there was almost full employment and, for some, more freedom and leisure time.

Britain after the Second World War

> German bombing raids had badly damaged all Britain's major cities. In London alone, 70,000 buildings had been destroyed and nearly 2 million damaged. There was a great need for reconstruction. There were also shortages in everything from houses to food.

> Many in Britain wanted society to change. The new Labour government, elected in 1945, began to create a welfare state as well as other changes. The NHS, British Rail, the new national rail network and London Transport all needed workers.

> Therefore, there were thousands of jobs available. However, in the years 1945–46 the British workforce fell by 1.38 million. This was due to deaths in combat, deaths from bombing, retirement, restrictions on married women working and emigration. Many people decided to emigrate, believing that they would have a better life in countries such as Canada or Australia. Between 1945 and 1960, nearly 1.5 million people left Britain.

> Parliament looked to the British Empire for workers. The British Nationality Act of 1948 gave everyone in the Commonwealth the right to live and work in Britain. Many in the Commonwealth, especially those in the Caribbean, felt a loyalty to Britain. They often regarded it as their 'mother country', for whom they had fought in two world wars. Furthermore, wages in Britain were at least three times higher than in the Caribbean. The 1948 Act appeared to be a wonderful opportunity, and thousands migrated from the Caribbean to work on rebuilding Britain.

Poverty and policing

In the decade after 1945, many in Britain lived in harsher conditions than during the war. For example:

- Thousands were waiting for new houses to be built.
- Bread was rationed for the first time and rationing of all foods didn't end until 1954.
- A severe winter in 1947 disrupted coal production and energy supplies, leading to further food shortages.

These problems were worse in London, which had the largest population and more homeless people than any other city.

Policing such a damaged country was very difficult, especially in London. Petty theft from damaged houses, offices and warehouses was common. Food and other goods were often sold secretly and illegally at high prices.

See page 27 for more on policing.

The Swinging Sixties

During the 1950s the economy gradually improved. Rationing ended and there was almost full employment.

In the 1960s London became the most exciting city in the world – the centre of new styles, fashion and music.

The 1960s were known as the 'Swinging Sixties'. Not everyone enjoyed the Swinging Sixties. There was still enormous poverty in areas such as the north-east of England. Poverty also affected many migrants.

Young people had more money, more leisure time and a greater sense of freedom than their parents.

Young people became politically aware and took part in marches and rallies. This political awareness affected black communities, too.

For more about black activism in Notting Hill in this period, see page 28.

Now try this

Give **three** reasons why migrants from the Caribbean moved to Britain after 1945.

Notting Hill

Notting Hill is an area of West London. After the Second World War, many Caribbean people migrated to Notting Hill. The area was very run down and housing was a major problem.

Why did Caribbean migrants settle in Notting Hill?

Paddington station is very close to Notting Hill. It was the first London station at which the trains carrying Caribbean migrants stopped. Caribbean officials waited there to welcome them and help them find accommodation.

Many migrants already had friends or family in Notting Hill and wanted to live near or with them. The black community in Notting Hill grew larger.

Few landlords elsewhere in London would rent houses or rooms to Caribbean migrants because of the colour of their skin.

The location of Notting Hill in London.

The hostile reaction of many white people made Caribbean migrants want to live close together.

The British government had advertised in the Caribbean for people to go to Britain to help rebuild the country. These migrants were known as 'the Windrush generation'.

Housing problems

- Caribbean migrants had to pay high rents for poor, squalid housing in Notting Hill.
- Landlords charged Caribbean people higher rents than white people for the same type of accommodation and so overcrowding was common.
- Few landlords made repairs to their houses as to spend money would reduce their profits.

Peter Rachman owned 80 run-down, squalid properties in Notting Hill. His houses were all HMOs and he charged high rents, making over £80,000 a year (nearly £2 million in today's money). He also had henchmen who intimidated tenants if they complained or couldn't pay their rent.

Slum landlords

- Houses in Notting Hill were often large but were usually cheap to buy because they were bomb-damaged.
- Many landlords applied to change the houses they owned into Houses of Multiple Occupancy (HMOs). This meant a single house could be rented to several people or even several families, not just to one family.
- Everyone in a single house shared a kitchen and a bathroom. These were often of poor quality.
- There were no rent controls so landlords could charge what they liked.

The Notting Hill Housing Trust

Bruce Kenrick was a minister in the United Reform Church. He lived in Notting Hill and was appalled by the conditions in which Caribbean families were forced to live. In 1965 he founded the Notting Hill Housing Trust, which aimed to provide decent houses at affordable rents to people in the community. By 1970 the Trust was housing nearly 1,000 people, improving people's lives.

Portobello Road Market

Portobello Road runs through the heart of Notting Hill. Caribbean migrants began to sell food such as yams and breadfruit, sweet potatoes and dasheen there, and the small market flourished. A cafe opened, serving Caribbean food.

In 1969 Island Records, founded in Jamaica, moved its base to near Portobello Road. The area soon gained a reputation as the place to go for Caribbean music and culture.

Now try this

Write a summary of how landlords took advantage of Caribbean migrants in Notting Hill.

Caribbean cultures

A rich Caribbean community began to develop in and influence Notting Hill. Here, migrants could live, work, enjoy familiar traditions and support one another.

How did Caribbean culture develop in Notting Hill?

Caribbean people's love of spicy, well-seasoned foods provided wonderful opportunities for traders to set up market stalls selling Caribbean food and ingredients for home cooking.

Some Caribbean migrants began setting up pubs, cafes and restaurants. For example, the *El Rio* cafe served good Caribbean food and was popular with new arrivals, quickly becoming a meeting place for the whole community.

Nightclubs and mainstream radio stations didn't play black music such as Blues, Reggae and Soul. It was therefore difficult for Caribbeans to access the music they wanted. However, Basing Street Studios opened in 1969 to meet this demand with performers such as Diana Ross.

The Mangrove restaurant.

HANDS OFF MANGROVE

The Metro Club opened in 1968. It was a community centre and youth club by day and a nightclub in the evenings. Young black people came from all over London and there were often large queues waiting to get in.

Many Caribbean people preferred to set up unofficial clubs, called *shebeens*, in their own homes and empty buildings. There they could smoke, drink and listen to Caribbean music. They used their own sound systems – and had to be careful the neighbours didn't complain.

There were lots of different Caribbean groups in Notting Hill, each with their own culture. This is one reason why Notting Hill became such a rich and vibrant community.

Caribbean residents, often living in cramped accommodation, needed clubs and centres where they could meet and it was from cafes, clubs and *shebeens* that they developed a sense of community.

The development of All Saints Road

All Saints Road became a centre of Caribbean culture and also of black activism.

- The *Mangrove*, opened in March 1968 by Frank Crichlow, was an all-night restaurant that served Caribbean food. It was the first black-owned restaurant in the area and was very popular – with people from within and outside the Caribbean community, as well as (black and white) celebrities.

- The headquarters of the activist group British Black Panthers was set up there in 1968.

- The *Apollo* was the first pub to serve black people.

- The Notting Hill Carnival organisers often met in the *Mangrove*.

See page 28 for more on the Mangrove and black activism.

Mutual self-help organisations

- The Caribbean community set up groups to help and support each other. These groups also helped give Caribbean migrants a clear sense of identity.

- **The London Free School** arranged childcare and organised activities for children. This was vital as many childminders refused to take black children.

- **The Unity Association** owned two properties where it housed homeless black youngsters who usually had great difficulty in finding housing.

- **The Black People's Information Centre** provided legal advice and welfare support. It also provided information on black history and civil rights.

- Some banks did not allow black people to open accounts and some building societies refused to give them a mortgage. **Pardner schemes** helped black people save so that they could buy their own homes.

Now try this

Choose **either** Caribbean food **or** Caribbean music. Describe how your choice was developed in Notting Hill and explain why it was important to Caribbean migrants.

Racism and policing

Racism was common throughout Britain in the years 1948 to 1970. Many black people were, for example, refused entry to pubs, restaurants and nightclubs. The Metropolitan Police, responsible for keeping law and order in Notting Hill, reflected racist attitudes held by many in Britain at that time. Consequently, they were not trusted by the black community. Police officers were mostly white and male. Black people who tried to join were rejected because of their colour.

Notting Hill riots, 1958

Racist tension and outbreaks of racially motivated violence were both common. The events of 1958 were by far the worst.

> On 30 August 1958 a mob of 400 white people, angered by seeing a mixed-race couple outside a pub, attacked the homes of Caribbean people. They used petrol bombs, iron bars, knuckle dusters and knives.

⬇

> Black people defended their homes. The riot lasted for 5 days before the police restored order.

⬇

> The rioting had an impact in several ways:
> - The police refused to accept that the riots were racially motivated.
> - The black community refused to accept that they had been involved in a riot. They claimed they were simply defending themselves and their property, not rioting.
> - Organisations were formed to fight for black civil rights. Among these were the Inter-Racial Friendship Coordinating Council and the West Indian Standing Conference.

The murder of Kelso Cochrane 1959

- On 17 May 1959 Kelso Cochrane, aged 32, was murdered by a gang of white youths. The murderers were never caught.

- People in the black community were angry, believing the police were too busy claiming the attack was not racist, instead of trying to catch the killers.

- Most newspapers agreed with the police. This further angered the black community, who were supported by a visit from the prime minister of Jamaica.

- Kelso Cochrane's funeral was attended by hundreds of white and black people, demonstrating support for the black community.

- Members of the Inter-Racial Friendship Coordinating Council asked the British prime minister to make racially motivated violence a crime. However, the government instead allowed the White Defence League to hold a rally in Trafalgar Square on 24 May 1959.

- Black people believed it was up to them to fight for civil rights.

Notting Hill became a focus for **anti-immigrant groups**, intent on stirring up fear among the migrant community. This fear was worsened because migrants didn't believe the police would protect them if a situation grew ugly.

The **Union Movement** was a far-right group led by Oswald Mosley. Its slogan was 'Keep Britain White' and it had offices in Notting Hill. These offices were deliberately established there in order to make the black community fearful.

The **White Defence League** was a violent organisation demanding Britain should be 'kept white'. Its office was in Notting Hill. It later joined with the British National Party – a move that was seen by the Caribbean community as provocative, intended to encourage violent acts against them.

Anti-immigrant groups

See page 20 for information on the British National Party.

Teddy boys roamed the streets looking for black people to attack. They were part of a gangland culture that flourished in Notting Hill, making it a dangerous place for Caribbean migrants.

In the 1959 general election Mosley ran for Parliament to win the seat of Kensington North, which included Notting Hill. In his violent and racist campaign, he falsely claimed amongst other things that black people were criminals and rapists. He only received 8.08% of the votes. He and the party never recovered from the defeat.

Now try this

Give **three** reasons why it was difficult to keep law and order in Notting Hill.

Black activism

In the Notting Hill area in the years c1948 to c1970, increased hostility led black activists to organise themselves to fight discrimination and racism.

Claudia Jones and the *West Indian Gazette*

Claudia Jones in the offices of the *West Indian Gazette*.

- Born in Trinidad, Claudia Jones was deported from the USA in 1955 (where she lived) because of her civil rights activities.
- She moved to Britain and in 1958 set up the *West Indian Gazette*, Britain's first major newspaper for black people.

In the 1950s, newspapers were one of the few ways of spreading information and ideas. With black communities suffering from racial discrimination and abuse, this 'voice' was very important to them.

- She persuaded London Transport to allow black people to rise to senior positions.
- She campaigned against the 1962 Commonwealth Immigration Act that restricted immigration from black, but not white, Commonwealth countries.
- Her offices in south London received sack-loads of abusive, often racist, mail.
- She persuaded the *West Indian Gazette* to sponsor the first Caribbean Carnival in 1959.

The Notting Hill Carnival

- The first Caribbean Carnival featured black entertainers such as Cleo Laine. It took place in St Pancras Town Hall, London, on 30 January 1959.
- Claudia Jones was instrumental in organising and running the first carnival. She then moved the event around England so that more people could get involved.
- In 1966, two years after Jones' death, the event moved outdoors. Now known as the Notting Hill Carnival, today it is the biggest street festival in Europe.

Frank Crichlow and the *Mangrove*

Police regularly raided the Mangrove looking for drugs. None were ever found.

⬇

Furious at police action (nine raids between January 1969 and July 1979), the British Black Panthers (BBP) helped organise a protest march.

⬇

The organisers told the Home Office, the prime minister, the leader of the opposition and Caribbean officials of their plan.

⬇

Over 150 people took part in the march on 9 August 1970. The police monitored the march and the Mangrove's customers.

⬇

The police claimed the marchers were inciting racial violence. Many were arrested, among them Frank Crichlow, the Mangrove's owner.

⬇

Magistrates dismissed the charges, but the Director of Public Prosecutions decided nine defendants (the Mangrove Nine) had to be tried, including Frank Crichlow.

⬇

All defendants were acquitted of the serious charges. The government tried to make the judge take back his ruling that there was racial hatred on both sides, but he refused. The trial was seen as a great victory for the black community.

The BBP, formed in 1968, campaigned against police brutality and on social issues. They aimed to build a sense of pride in the black community. Their leaders included Obi Egbuna, Darcus Howe, Altheia Jones-LeCointe and Olive Morris. (Howe and Jones-LeCointe were part of the Mangrove Nine.) By the early 1970s the BBP had about 3,000 members and worked with other groups tackling racism.

Now try this

Write a summary explaining the importance of the *West Indian Gazette* to the Caribbean community of Notting Hill.

Exam overview

This page outlines you to the main features and requirements of the Paper 1 Option 13 exam paper.

About Paper 1

- Paper 1 is for assessing both your thematic study (Section B) as well as your study of a historic environment (Section A).
- Section A will be on **Notting Hill, c1948–c1970**.
- Section B will be on **Migrants in Britain, c800–present**.
- You will receive two documents: a question paper, which you write into, and a sources booklet, which you will need for Section A.

The Paper 1 exam lasts for 1 hour and 15 minutes (75 minutes) in total. You should spend about 25 minutes on the historic environment and about 50 minutes on the thematic study.

The questions

You can see examples of all the question types on pages 30–38. You can practise answering these question types on pages 39–56.

The question for Paper 1 will always follow the same pattern.

Section A: Question 1

Describe **two** features of…   **(4 marks)**

> Question 1 targets AO1. AO1 is about showing your **knowledge** and **understanding** of key features and characteristics of the topic.

Section A: Question 2(a)

How useful are Sources A and B for an enquiry about…?

Explain your answer, using Sources A and B and your knowledge of the historical context.   **(8 marks)**

> Question 2(a) targets AO3, which is about analysing, evaluating and using sources to make judgements. This is where you show your ability to **analyse** and **evaluate** the usefulness of **sources**.

Section A: Question 2(b)

How could you follow up Source [A/B] to find out more about…?   **(4 marks)**

Complete the table, giving the question you would ask and the type of source you could use.

> Question 2(b) also targets AO3. This is where you show your ability to use **sources** to frame historical questions.

Section B: Question 3

Explain **one** way in which… was similar to/ different from…   **(4 marks)**

> Question 3 targets both AO1 and AO2. AO2 is about explaining and analysing key events using historical concepts, such as causation, consequence, change, continuity, similarity and difference. This question focuses on **similarity** or **difference** across time.

Section B: Question 4

Explain why…   **(12 marks)**

Two prompts and your own information.

> Question 4 also targets both AO1 and AO2. It focuses on causation, which means explaining why something happened. The question will be focused on the process of change.

Section B: Question 5 or 6

'Statement'. How far do you agree?

Explain your answer.   **(16 marks plus 4 marks for SPaG and use of specialist terminology)**

Two prompts and your own information.

> You should choose **either** Question 5 **or** Question 6. They both target AO1 and AO2. You need to make a **judgement** about how far you agree with the statement in the question. There are up to 4 marks available for spelling, punctuation and grammar (SPaG) and use of specialist terminology.

Question 1: Describing features

Question 1 on your exam paper will ask you to 'Describe **two** features of...' something from the content of the historic environment (Notting Hill, c1948–c1970). There are four marks available for this question, two for each feature you describe.

Worked example

Describe **two** features of the development of All Saints Road in Notting Hill.   (4 marks)

What does 'describe' mean?

Describe means to give an account of the main features or characteristics of something. You must develop the description with relevant details, but you do not need to include reasons or justifications.

🔗 **Links** You can revise the development of All Saints Road on page 26.

Sample answer

Feature 1
Black businessmen began setting up businesses in All Saints Road.

Feature 2
Caribbean people also set up unofficial clubs, called 'shebeens'. There they would drink and listen to Caribbean music.

This is a feature, but it needs development. For example, you could add detail mentioning an example of a business that was set up.

Make sure you read the question carefully. It is asking for features of the development of All Saints Road, not for information about Caribbean cultures in general.

Improved answer

Feature 1
Black businessmen began setting up businesses in All Saints Road. This included 'The Mangrove', which became a meeting place for members of the British Black Panthers.

Feature 2
All Saints Road became a centre for Caribbean cultures. Many shops and restaurants specialised in Caribbean food.

This is the same feature as above, but now it has been improved with additional detail that is an example of one of the businesses.

This is a second feature. It is different from Feature 1, and it has been developed with additional detail.

Top hints for a successful answer

- Make sure that you describe **two different features**, rather than describing the same feature twice.
- Make sure that both features relate to the specific topic in the question.
- Write two sentences for each feature – one to identify the feature, and a second sentence to add supporting information.
- Use the spaces on the exam paper to organise your answer.
- Be specific and avoid vague or general sentences. For example, saying 'All Saints Road gained a reputation for Caribbean music' is specific, but 'some people liked All Saints Road' is too general – **who** liked it and **what** did they like?

Source skills 1

In your exam, Questions 2(a) and 2(b) are based upon **sources**. Question 2(a) will ask you about the **usefulness** of the sources and Question 2(b) will ask you how you would **follow up** information in one source.

Usefulness

'Usefulness' means how valuable the sources are for the enquiry. These three points can help you make a judgement about usefulness.

1 **Content**

- What information in the sources is relevant to the enquiry?
- How useful is this information?

> You could underline and annotate information in the source to help with this.

> Remember that this is not necessarily about the amount of information in a source. No source can mention everything and even a small piece of information can be useful.

2 **Provenance**

- Nature: the type of source it is.
- Origins: who produced it and when.
- Purpose: the reason the source was created.
- How do these things impact on the usefulness of the source?

> Make sure that you link these points to how useful the source is. Remember that an unreliable source can still be useful.

3 **Context**

- Use your own knowledge of the enquiry topic to evaluate the source.
- Is the information in the source accurate compared with what you know?

> Think about whether the author of the source has deliberately chosen or missed out any information. **Why** might they have chosen or missed out the information? **How** does this affect the usefulness?

Following up sources

For Question 2(b) you have to complete a table like the one below.

> The detail you pick should be related to the enquiry in the question.

Detail in Source [A/B] that I would follow up:

....

Question I would ask:

....

What type of source I could use:

....

How this might help answer my question:

....

> The question should be related to the enquiry in the question **and** the details you've written above.

> There are many types of source, but you need to choose one that will really help you to answer the question you asked above.

> Write one or two sentences explaining how the source you have chosen above could help you answer your question.

Examples of sources: national

- Articles in national newspapers
- Government records
- Television reports
- Opinion polls.

Examples of sources: local

- Publications written for the Caribbean community
- Local council or police records
- Housing and employment records
- Oral or written memoirs by local residents.

Source skills 2

In your exam you will be given a **source booklet** containing **two** sources. Both Questions 2(a) and 2(b) require you to **analyse** the sources so it is important that you spend time reading and looking at these sources carefully before you start your answers. You can also annotate the sources to help you.

Source A: A photograph of a young Caribbean immigrant looking for accommodation in London 1958. The sign on the door, which reads 'Rooms to let, no coloured men', was placed there by the property owner. The photograph was taken by a journalist working for a press agency.

Don't forget to read the information **about** the source. It is where you'll find vital information on the **provenance** (nature, origin and purpose) of the source.

It can be hard to assess the purpose of a photo or an illustration. Read the provenance carefully to help with your assessment.

How could the fact that the photo was taken by a journalist for a press agency affect its usefulness?

Look at the date of the source. Does the source agree with what you know about housing in Notting Hill at this time?

Image sources need studying just as carefully as text sources. What can you see in the image? What is the photographer trying to convey? How useful is this to the enquiry?

The date 1963 is given. How does the content of the source match what you know about housing in Notting Hill around this time?

The fact that the article was written to expose the situation might indicate that the newspaper has selected evidence to emphasise the problems, potentially making it less useful as a balanced evaluation of the situation.

The provenance gives information about where the source is from. How does this affect its usefulness?

Source B: From an article about housing in Notting Hill, published in the newspaper *The People*. It was published in 1963 as an exposé on the landlord Peter Rachman. Rachman had died in 1962.

> The flood of West Indian immigrants to Britain was at its height. Rachman soon found that he could make fantastic money if he could force out white families and pack each room with seven or eight immigrants. And even greater profits could be made by putting prostitutes into the rooms… Rachman would pack every room in the house with coloured people – often two, three or four to one room, and each individual paying rent… The houses were controlled for him by a gang of strong-arm thugs and a team of rent collectors who turned Alsatian dogs on anyone who refused to pay the rents demanded.

When you're reading the source, highlight any particularly useful information it gives that is relevant to the enquiry.

Question 2(a): Usefulness of sources

Question 2(a) on your exam paper will ask you about how useful two sources are for a particular enquiry. There are eight marks available for this question.

Worked example

Study Sources A and B on page 33.

How useful are Sources A and B for an enquiry into the problems of housing for migrants to Notting Hill, c1948–c1970?

Explain your answer, using Sources A and B and your knowledge of the historical context.

(8 marks)

What does 'how useful' mean?

How useful means how valuable the sources for a specific enquiry are. You need to come to a judgement about how useful each of the sources is for the enquiry in the question.

Watch out!

'How useful' is not the same as how reliable a source is. A source can be unreliable but still useful.

 Links You can revise housing on page 25.

Sample extract

Source A is a photograph of an immigrant from the Caribbean searching for accommodation. It is fairly useful as it shows a major problem faced by black immigrants – finding accommodation. The photo shows the man with his bags, which indicates that he has no current accommodation, but the sign on the door reads 'No coloured men'. This is useful in indicating that not all landlords were willing to rent to people from the Caribbean.

The caption indicates that this was taken in 1958, which was during the period of mass migration from the Caribbean in the 1950s. Notting Hill was one of the few places where landlords would rent to black people, so many black people were forced to find accommodation there even though properties were often overcrowded and poorly maintained. Therefore, this picture is useful as it is representative of an experience faced by many migrants.

Since the media in the later 1950s were interested in reporting on the racial tensions in Notting Hill, it is possible that it was deliberately taken or even staged to emphasise the problems faced by black immigrants. Even though this makes it less reliable, it is still fairly useful in showing that the British public were aware of the problems that immigrants from the Caribbean were facing.

Source B describes the problems faced by immigrants…

Always make a **judgement** on how useful a source is and then explain how you have reached this decision. This answer has done this by saying that it is 'fairly useful' for showing the problem of finding accommodation.

With image sources refer to details in the source to support your answer. With text sources, use short quotes.

Use your **own knowledge** of the topic to analyse the source – this answer shows contextual awareness of the reasons why so many Caribbean immigrants found accommodation in Notting Hill.

It is important to include why the source was made. When mentioning purpose or reliability, it is important to link this to how it affects the usefulness of the source.

You **must** use both sources in your answer, so it is good that this student is continuing their answer by writing about Source B. Remember that the question **does not** require you to compare the sources.

Question 2(b): Following up sources

Question 2(b) on your exam paper will ask you to pick a detail from one source and explain how you would follow up that detail in another source. There are four marks available for this question.

Worked example

Study Source B on page 32.

How could you follow up Source B to find out more about the problems of housing for migrants to Notting Hill, c1948–c1970?

In your answer, you must give the question you would ask and the type of source you could use.

Complete the table below.　　**(4 marks)**

What does 'follow up' mean?

Follow up means investigate something further. In other words, if you were a historian investigating this enquiry, how you could find out more information on something in the source by using another source.

This question will **either** ask about Source A **or** Source B. Check carefully which one it is asking about.

 **Links**　You can revise housing on page 25.

Sample answer

Detail in Source B that I would follow up:

'packed each room with seven or eight immigrants'.

Question I would ask:

How many different rooms were usually rented out in each house?

What type of source I could use:

Local council housing inspection records.

How this might help answer my question:

The records would indicate how many different rooms were in the inspected properties.

The answer space has a table for you to structure your answer.

Identify **one** specific detail from the content of the source. This could be a short quote from a text source, or a detail you can see in an image.

Make sure the question you choose is linked to the detail you selected, as well as to the enquiry in the question.

Remember, you only need to give one type of source here. Be specific – saying 'a newspaper' or 'a letter' is too general. But there is only one mark for each point, so don't go into more detail than is necessary.

The last stage requires one or two sentences. Say how the source you have chosen could be used to answer the question you selected.

Remember!

Questions 2(a) and 2(b) will always have the **same** enquiry focus. In both questions, it is very important to write answers that relate to the enquiry focus, not just the topic of Notting Hill in general.

Question 3: Making comparisons

Question 3 on your exam paper will ask you to explain one way in which something was similar or different over time. There are four marks available for this question.

Worked example

Explain **one** way in which reasons for migration to Britain in the 16th century were similar to reasons for migration to Britain in the 20th century.

(4 marks)

What does 'explain one way' mean?

Explain one way means providing details of one way in which something was similar or **different** over time. You do not need to explain the reasons for the similarity or difference, just **how** they were.

Links   You can revise the reasons for migration on pages 7 and 19.

Sample answer

In the 16th century, French Protestants called Huguenots came to England. One of the reasons that they came to England was to escape religious persecution. This was because the development of Protestantism in Europe had led to religious conflict with the Catholic Church. Many French Protestants believed that England was a safe place because the Church of England had broken from the Roman Catholic Church.

This was different to some migrants in the 20th century. They came because of EU trade laws, which allowed them to legally move to find work. Also, some migrants moved to Britain because the British government encouraged them to help rebuild Britain after the war.

Although this answer does identify a reason for the Huguenot migration to Britain, it is not focused on the question. The answer should explain how this reason was **similar** to the reasons for migration in the 20th century.

This is about a difference, but the question asks about a similarity. Always check the question carefully to see if it is about similarities or differences. You could underline the word in the question to help you focus.

As well as focusing on differences, not similarities, this answer has made more than one comparison. The question only asks for one.

Improved answer

A similarity was that migrants in both centuries came to Britain because of religious persecution. In the 16th century, the Huguenots came to England because they were Protestants and faced persecution in France from the Catholic Church, as well as from the government. This is similar to the reason for Jewish people from Europe migrating to Britain in the 20th century. Jews faced persecution and violence led by the Nazi government in Germany. The 'Kindertransport' arranged for Jewish children to be sent to Britain, which was still seen as a safe place, just as it had been in the 16th century.

This answer has started by identifying the similarity. This can help to focus the answer. The answer gives just one similarity.

The answer has a specific example from each period which has been used to support the comparison.

Did you notice that the improved answer is shorter than the sample answer? The question is only worth four marks, so long answers are not required. Avoid writing too much so that you have time for the questions worth more marks.

Question 4: Explaining why

Question 4 on your exam paper is about causation, which means **explaining why** something happened. It will always cover a period of 100 years or more. There are 12 marks available for this question.

Worked example

Explain why migrants from Europe were able to settle successfully in Britain in the 16th and 17th centuries.

You **may** use the following in your answer:
- the impact of migrants in banking
- draining marshland

You **must** also use information of your own.

(12 marks)

What does 'explain why' mean?

Explain why means saying **why** something happened, backed up with examples to support the reasons you give. The focus in this question will be about the process of change. A good way to get into an explanation is to use sentence starters such as 'One reason for this was...' or 'This was because...'.

The bullet points in the question are only suggestions and you don't have to use them. However, you **must** include information of your own in your answer.

Links You can revise the settlement of migrants in early modern Britain on pages 7–11.

Sample extract

There were many migrants who settled successfully in Britain in the 16th and 17th centuries. One group was migrants from Africa. For example, there were African migrants working as sailors, servants and weavers. It was fashionable for wealthy families in the 17th century to have a black child servant.

The Huguenots became involved in banking in Britain. They invested in the Bank of England when it was founded in 1684. This was helpful for the British government, who borrowed this money to fight wars to expand the British Empire. The Huguenots did better at settling than the Irish in the 19th century.

This student has used their own knowledge – migrants from Africa were not mentioned in the prompts. But they have described the migration, rather than explaining why migrants settled successfully.

This is not answering the question. Instead of saying how the British government used the money, it would be better to say how banking helped the migrants to settle successfully.

This example is not from the period in the question. Always use examples from the right period.

Improved extract

One reason that migrants were successful in settling is that they became involved in banking. The Huguenots invested heavily in the Bank of England when it was founded in 1684. This made them valuable to the British government, which relied on the Bank of England for loans to pay for their wars. Because they strengthened the economy, the Huguenots were seen as a valuable addition to British society.

Another reason was that...

The paragraph starts with a clear statement, which makes it easier to write in a focused and analytical way.

The paragraph has a specific example to support the reason.

The paragraph is focused on the question by explaining why migrants settled successfully.

You should aim to give **three** reasons, so it is good to see that the answer is continuing with another reason.

Question 5/6: Making a judgement 1

On the exam paper, you will choose to answer **either** Question 5 **or** Question 6. Both involve **analysing the statement** in the question and deciding how far you agree with it. There are 16 marks available (20 when you include SPaG) for this question. It has two prompts to help you, but you **must** also use information of your own.

Worked example

'The impact on land ownership was the most important consequence of migration to England during the years c800–c1500.'

How far do you agree? Explain your answer.

> You **may** use the following in your answer:
> - the feudal system
> - laws
>
> You **must** also use information of your own.

(16 marks plus 4 marks for SPaG and use of specialist terminology)

Analysing the statement

The statement will **always** give a judgement on something. You decide whether you agree or not by weighing up points that support the statement with points that oppose it. It is important to make a final judgement.

Pay attention to the dates in the question, and only use examples from that period. Questions 5 and 6 will always cover a period of 200 years or more.

Links You can revise the consequences of migration on page 4.

Sample answer

In the years c800–c1500, migration had several consequences in England. Changes to land ownership were significant, but not as important as other changes, especially the development of the wool trade.

Land ownership changed when the Vikings settled in large parts of Britain. In 1016, when the Saxons surrendered to Cnut, he set up new earldoms such as Wessex, with powerful Saxon nobles who he could trust to rule each one. The Normans who settled made even bigger changes to land ownership. William I introduced the feudal system. He took 30% of the land for himself, gave 25% to the Church and then shared what was left with his followers in return for oaths of loyalty. This had completely changed land ownership in England by the 1100s as it was all indirectly owned by the king and his trusted followers. Previously it had been owned by a large number of Saxon landowners. This shows that changes to land ownership were an important consequence of migration.

Although changes to land ownership were important, other changes were even more important. One example of this is the changes to laws. The Vikings introduced their own laws

The answer has a short introduction which helps by starting the answer off with a clear argument. Introductions should not be long.

The answer has specific examples which are used to support the changes in land ownership which were a consequence of migration.

Each example is linked clearly to the point of land ownership.

Having written about the examples that support the statement, the answer starts to consider examples that challenge the statement. This is clear because it says 'Although changes to land ownership were important, other changes were even more important.'

Question 5/6: Making a judgement 2

Sample answer continued

to the parts of England under Danelaw. For example, under the Viking laws, women had almost equal rights with men. The Normans later introduced laws that affected many Saxons. An example is the Forest Laws, which created royal forests, where the king controlled hunting. A second example is 'murdrum', which was a fine on Saxons if a Norman was murdered and the murderer was not caught. These laws affected communities in England by changing traditions and customs. This was an important consequence of migration.

Another important change was an increase in trade. Under the Normans, many traders from Europe settled in English ports and towns, which was good for the economy. Additionally, William I encouraged Jewish moneylenders to migrate to England. In the 13th century, Henry III encouraged bankers from Italy to move to England. These businessmen loaned money to nobles, but also to merchants, who used it to expand their trade. In the 14th and 15th centuries, kings encouraged Flemish weavers to migrate to England to strengthen the cloth trade. They also encouraged Hansa merchants to set up a trading centre in London. The impact of these groups of migrants was to strengthen the economy in England and encourage growth in towns and ports. This was an important consequence of migration.

Overall, the impact of migrants on land ownership in England in the years c800–c1500 was important because it led to far greater royal control of land. But for many peasants, life did not change very much with land ownership changes. More important were the changes to laws and trade, which directly affected the lives of people in England. These changes, like the legal rights of women and the growth of wealth in the towns and ports, affected the daily lives of far more people than the changes of land ownership did.

Remember that there are 4 marks available for spelling, punctuation, grammar and use of technical language. So, it is better to use technical language, such as 'Danelaw', than say 'areas where Danes were in control'.

The answer uses specific examples to support the points. For example, here it mentions the Forest Laws.

Trade was not mentioned in the question. It is important to use your own information and not just rely on the two bullet points.

The paragraphs in this answer are PEEL paragraphs – point, evidence, explain, link. They start by identifying a point, then give evidence, then explain what the significance is, and then link back to the question.

You should try to cover the whole period in the question with your examples. Earlier in the answer there was information about the Vikings and Normans, and this paragraph mentions the 14th and 15th centuries.

The answer makes a **final judgement** about how far the student agrees with the statement in the question. The judgement is supported by a short but clear reason for the decision that has been reached. The judgement has been made on the basis of how far the changes affected people's lives.

Practice

Put your skills and knowledge into practice with the following question.

Option 13: Migrants in Britain, c800–present *and* Notting Hill, c1948–c1970

SECTION A: Notting Hill, c1948–c1970

Answer Questions 1 and 2.

1   Describe **two** features of the British Black Panthers.

(4 marks)

Feature 1

Guided   The British Black Panthers were formed to

fight for racial equality...

....

....

....

....

Feature 2

....

....

....

....

....

You have to answer all questions in Section A. It is a good idea to spend about 25 minutes on this section so that you have time to complete Section B.

Links You can revise the British Black Panthers on page 28.

For this question, you need to identify **two** different features, and develop each feature with a relevant detail. The example given for Feature 1 has not yet been developed.

Your exam paper will have a separate space for each feature. Use the spaces to organise your answer.

Describe means you have to identify a main characteristic of the subject and support it with an additional detail. You do **not** need to explain **why** the feature was important.

You can see that the answer space for this question is not very large. This is because you do not need to write a lot – the question is only worth 4 marks. By not writing too much, you can save time for the questions that have more marks.

Practice

Put your skills and knowledge into practice with the following question.

2 (a) Study Sources A and B on page 56.

How useful are Sources A and B for an enquiry into the murder of Kelso Cochrane (1959)?

Explain your answer, using Sources A and B and your own knowledge of the historical context. **(8 marks)**

....

....

....

....

....

....

....

....

....

....

....

....

....

....

....

....

....

....

....

....

....

....

Read the question carefully. Then, before starting to answer, spend some time studying and annotating the sources.

You can find some hints about annotating sources on page 32.

Links You can revise the murder of Kelso Cochrane on page 27.

You could make a brief plan to help you organise the points you want to mention.

Make sure you use **both** sources in your answer. You should come to a judgement about how useful each source is.

Make sure that you focus on the usefulness of the sources **for the enquiry in the question** – the murder of Kelso Cochrane.

Remember to include the key things for each source: the content, the provenance and your own knowledge. This all needs to be linked to how useful the source is for the enquiry.

On page 32 you can find some suggestions to help you to assess the usefulness of the content and provenance of a source.

In Source A, the police statements emphasise that the murder was not connected to racism. Think about what you know about racial tensions in Notting Hill in the period shortly before 1959. Is there something that could explain why the police were so keen to persuade people that it was **not** about racism? How does this affect the usefulness of the source?

Practice

Use this page to continue your answer to Question 2(a).

....
....
....
....
....
....
....
....
....
....
....
....
....
....
....
....
....
....
....
....
....
....
....
....
....
....

Remember that no source can mention everything, so avoid listing things that the source does not mention unless you think it was missed out on purpose. Missing information usually only affects the usefulness of a source if it was missed out deliberately, for example to make something sound better or worse than it really was.

For Source B, you could say that it is useful in showing the significant consequences of the murder of Kelso Cochrane in the black community. This comment would be based on the fact that Source B shows protesters still outside government buildings in London in June 1959, even though the murder happened in May 1959. This uses the content, as well as a piece of contextual own knowledge about the murder to judge the usefulness.

Have you used some of your own knowledge with **both** the sources? Assess whether the source is accurate and balanced by using your knowledge of the topic and say how that affects the usefulness.

Don't forget that the question has an enquiry focus. Does your answer explain the usefulness for the specific enquiry, rather than look at Notting Hill in general?

Make sure that everything you mention – whether the content, the provenance or your own knowledge – is linked to **how useful** the source is.

Remember, you don't need to compare the two sources. You can judge each one separately.

Practice

Put your skills and knowledge into practice with the following question.

2 (b) Study Source B on page 56.

How could you follow up Source B to find out more about the murder of Kelso Cochrane (1959)?

In your answer, you must give the question you would ask and the type of source you could use.

Complete the table below. **(4 marks)**

Detail in Source B that I would follow up:

....

....

....

Question I would ask:

....

....

....

What type of source I could use:

....

....

....

How this might help answer my question:

....

....

....

....

🔗 **Links** You can revise the murder of Kelso Cochrane on page 27.

Pick a relevant detail from the source. Because this one is a picture, you need to choose something you can see.

Your question needs to connect to the enquiry in the question, but it also needs to connect to the detail you picked. If you can't connect your question to both, pick a different detail.

You need to pick a specific source that would be useful to answer your question. It could be a local or national source, but it can't be too general — for example, 'a newspaper' is too general.

There are a few examples of the types of sources you could choose on page 31.

Say how the source you picked in the third step would help you answer the question you wrote in the second step. 'It would tell me what I want to know' is too general!

Remember!
This question is only worth four marks, so use the spaces and keep your answers short, but specific.

Practice

Put your skills and knowledge into practice with the following question.

SECTION B: Migrants in Britain, c800–present

Answer Questions 3 AND 4. Then answer EITHER Question 5 OR 6.

3 Explain **one** way in which the experiences of Huguenot migrants in the 17th century were different from the experiences of Jewish migrants in the 19th century.

(4 marks)

....

....

....

....

....

....

....

....

....

....

....

....

....

If you spent 25 minutes on Section A, you will have 50 minutes left to complete this section. It is a good idea to try to use the last 5 minutes for checking your answers.

In the exam, this question could be about a similarity **or** a difference. This question is about a **difference**.

🔗 **Links** You can revise the experience of the Huguenots in the 17th century on page 11, and the experience of Jewish migrants in the 19th century on pages 14 and 17.

Remember to give **one** difference only, as the question asks. For example, you could focus on how the Huguenots' religious beliefs were accepted because they shared ideas with British Protestantism, whereas many Jews faced persecution because of their religious practices, which were different to those of the Christian population.

Remember!

You **don't** need to explain why they were different – just **how**! The question is only worth four marks, so don't spend too much time answering it. You will need time on the longer questions on the next pages.

Once you have identified the difference, it is important to include a relevant example from **both** of the periods in the question. If the question mentions specific groups of migrants, like this one does, your supporting information must be about them.

Practice

Put your skills and knowledge into practice with the following question.

4 Explain why there was economic growth in England during the 16th and 17th centuries.

> You **may** use the following in your answer:
> - Flemish migrants
> - global trading companies
>
> You **must** also use information of your own.

(12 marks)

....

....

....

....

....

Guided   The first reason for economic growth was that

global trading companies expanded England's international

trade. For example, in 1600, Queen Elizabeth issued a charter

to set up the East India Company, which traded cotton, silk

and spices. In 1660 Charles II issued a charter to set up the

Company of Royal Adventurers Trading to Africa, which traded

gold, silver and enslaved Africans. These companies brought

expensive luxury goods to Britain, and the transatlantic slave

trade in particular brought investors huge amounts of money

– at the cost of human misery. For this reason, global trading

companies caused economic growth in England.

....

....

....

....

The question will have dates covering at least 100 years. You could highlight or underline the dates so that you don't forget and use examples from the wrong period. Remember that the 16th century was the 1500s, and the 17th century was the 1600s.

The two bullet points are suggestions of what you could mention. But you **must** also add some of your own information.

 Links   You can revise the economic growth of England on page 6, and the role of migrants in the economic growth on pages 9–11.

It is a good idea to make **a brief plan** at the top of the answer space before you start writing, so that you can choose the different reasons that you will write about. This could simply be a list of three reasons.

You **don't** need to start this question with an introduction. You can just start with the first reason.

This is written as a **PEEL paragraph**, which makes the reason clear. PEEL means point, evidence, explain and link. In the first line the **point**, or reason, is identified. Then **evidence** is used. After that the reason is **explained** to say why it caused economic growth. Then the question is **linked** back to the question.

This question asks you to explain **why** there was economic growth, rather than simply describe the economic growth. Focus on three separate reasons.

You could make your answer clearer by starting each paragraph with a phrase like 'The first reason was...' or 'Another reason was...'.

Practice

Use this page to continue your answer to Question 4.

....

....

....

....

....

....

....

....

....

....

....

....

....

....

....

....

....

....

....

....

....

....

....

....

....

....

....

....

A useful phrase to avoid describing is 'This meant that...'. You could also use other analytical words and phrases such as 'As a result...', 'Consequently...' or 'This increased/reduced...'.

Remember that you need to explain **why** each reason caused the change or development in the question. In this question, why did each reason cause economic growth?

Use **key terms** in your answer, such as names, dates and examples.

Check your answer carefully – are all the examples you have used from the years c1500–c1700?

Have you included your **own knowledge**, which is not part of the two bullet points, in the question? For example, the Huguenots played an important role in the economy in this period and they are not mentioned in the question.

Keep an eye on the time. Although you need to spend longer on this question than the earlier questions because it is worth 12 marks, remember that you need to leave enough time for the last question which is worth 20 marks. Focus on **three good reasons**, rather than writing everything you know.

There is no need to write a conclusion for this question because this question does **not** require you to make a judgement.

Remember!

Just because this question has so much space to answer, it does not mean you have to use it all. Writing a well-supported and clear answer with three good reasons is better than writing a very long answer.

Practice

Use this page to continue your answer to Question 4.

....

....

....

....

....

....

....

....

....

....

....

....

....

....

....

....

....

....

....

....

....

....

....

....

....

....

....

....

Practice

Put your skills and knowledge into practice with the following questions.

You need to choose whether you will answer Question 5 **or** Question 6. Each option is worth the same number of marks. Even if one of the questions looks like one you can answer, read them both carefully and choose the one that you think is right for you.

Answer EITHER Question 5 OR Question 6.

Spelling, punctuation, grammar and use of specialist terminology will be assessed in this question.

EITHER

5 'Warfare was the main reason for successful settlement in Britain during the middle ages.'

How far do you agree? Explain your answer.

> You **may** use the following in your answer:
> • Norman invaders
> • European craftsmen
> You **must** also use information of your own.

(16 marks, plus 4 marks for SPaG)

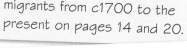 **Links** You can revise the reasons for successful settlement in Britain during the middle ages on page 2.

This is telling you that there will be marks awarded for your use of **SPaG** and specialist terminology.

OR

6 'Poor living conditions were the greatest challenge faced by migrants in Britain in the period c1700–present.'

How far do you agree? Explain your answer.

> You **may** use the following in your answer:
> • slum housing
> • sweatshops
> You **must** also use information of your own.

(16 marks, plus 4 marks for SPaG)

 Links You can revise the experiences of migrants from c1700 to the present on pages 14 and 20.

The two bullet points are suggestions for what you could use to answer the question. You must also use information of your own.

Each option is worth 20 marks – 16 marks for the answer and 4 marks for SPaG and use of specialist terminology.

In the exam, you will have one space to answer the question you have chosen. In this book, there are two spaces, so that you can have a go at both of the questions. To answer Question 5, turn to page 48, and to answer Question 6, turn to page 52.

Choosing a question

At the top of the answer space for Questions 5 and 6, there is a space for you to indicate which question you have chosen. Mark a cross in the box for the question you are answering.

If you change your mind or you have marked the wrong box, don't worry. Just put a line through the cross, and then put a cross in the other box.

What is SPaG (spelling, punctuation, grammar) and use of specialist terminology?

• Spelling means writing the words correctly.

• Punctuation means using full stops, commas and other punctuation marks correctly.

• Grammar means writing sentences and paragraphs that make sense.

• Specialist terminology means using historical words, such as names, places, events and concepts.

Practice

Use this page to start your answer to Question 5.

Indicate which question you are answering by marking a cross in the box. If you change your mind, put a line through the box and then indicate your new question with a cross.

Chosen question number: **Question 5** ☒   **Question 6** ☐

....

....

....

....

....

....

....

....

....

(**Guided**)   Warfare was an important reason for people

successfully settling in Britain during the middle ages,

for example the Vikings and the Normans. But there were

other reasons that were more important, such as trade

and seeking work.

....

....

....

....

....

....

....

This is where you would indicate whether you are answering Question 5 or 6. Question 5 has been marked to show you how to do it.

You should start your answer with a plan. This helps to keep your answer organised. List factors that support the statement and ones that challenge the statement. For example:

Support	Against
Viking warriors settled as part of the Great Army to conquer and settle in Britain.	Jewish and Christian moneylenders settled successfully because merchants and the king needed their services.
In 1066, Norman invaders conquered England, which allowed them to settle.	Workers from Europe, e.g. Flemish weavers, were welcomed as they carried out skilled and labouring work.

You can write the plan at the start of the answer space.

This is an example of an introduction to start the answer. It is short, but it identifies the overall judgement that the answer will give. This can help to start the answer analytically.

You could start the first side of your argument by saying 'Some migrants settled successfully because of warfare.' Then you can support this with your examples.

It is a good idea to write PEEL paragraphs (point, evidence, explain, link).

Practice

Use this page to continue your answer to Question 5.

....

....

....

....

....

....

....

....

....

....

....

....

....

....

....

....

....

....

....

....

....

....

....

Make sure that in the answer you have examples that cover the **full range** of c800–c1500 (the middle ages), rather than only using examples from one part of the period.

Support your point with specific examples. For example, you could refer to a specific group, such as the Flemish weavers.

Remember that your answer should be focused on the reasons for successful settlement, not just describing migration in the middle ages.

It is important to make a **judgement** at the end of your answer. How far do you agree or disagree with the statement in the question overall? Was the main reason for successful settlement in the middle ages warfare, or was it something else?

Once you have made your judgement, you need to give a **reason** for your decision. For example, you might have based your judgement on the number of people affected by the reason you chose, or the number of years it was relevant for, or because the reason you have chosen was a fundamental cause behind the other reasons for successful settlement.

There are four marks for SPaG, so when you are checking through your exam paper in the last five minutes, it is important to look for any mistakes in spelling and grammar in your answer.

Practice

Use this page to continue your answer to Question 5.

Practice

Use this page to continue your answer to Question 5.

Practice

Use this page to start your answer to Question 6.

Indicate which question you are answering by marking a cross in the box. If you change your mind, put a line through the box and then indicate your new question with a cross.

Chosen question number: **Question 5** ☐   **Question 6** ☒

This is where you would indicate whether you are answering Question 5 or 6. Question 6 has been marked to show you how to do it.

A good way to write an organised answer is to start with a plan. Your plan could be in any style that helps you to organise your points. You can write the plan at the start of the answer space. Here are some examples of points to include:

Support	Against
Irish immigrants often lived in poor, run-down areas, e.g. in parts of Liverpool.	Problems over work, e.g. the conditions in sweatshops and docks.
Jewish immigrants to London often ended up in poor accommodation in the 1800s.	Racial tensions, e.g. anti-Semitic media reports and violence in the 1800s.
Landlords in the mid-1900s often refused to rent to immigrants who were not white.	Legal problems, e.g. problems faced by the Windrush generation to prove their right to stay in the UK.

Guided   Immigrants to Britain in the years c1700–c1900

faced many challenges. Housing was a constant problem,

but there were more serious challenges that they faced,

especially racial tensions and problems with work.

This short introduction identifies what your answer will be about and it indicates the overall judgement. This helps to avoid describing the topic.

Pay attention to the dates in the question. It says 'c1700–present', so avoid using examples from before c1700 as they are not relevant.

Using PEEL paragraphs (point, evidence, explain, link) is one way of organising your answer and keeping yourself focused on writing analytically.

Practice

Use this page to continue your answer to Question 6.

....

....

....

....

....

....

....

....

....

....

....

....

....

....

....

....

....

....

....

....

....

....

....

....

Try using some of these phrases to help you to write **analytically**, instead of just describing the problems faced by immigrants:
- This caused problems because...
- The impact of this was...
- As a result...
- This increased (or decreased)...

To support the statement in the question, use examples where migrants faced problems with housing in the years c1700–present.

Use examples that cover the date range in the question. You need examples from the years c1700–c1900 as well as from c1900–present. If your examples only cover part of the period, you are not fully answering the question.

Use **specialist terms** in your answer, such as names, events and historical developments.

You need to make a **judgement** about how far you agree that problems with housing were the biggest challenge for immigrants. Give a reason, and then support it with a reason. The reason could be, for example, because of how hard it was to solve the problem, how long it lasted for, how many immigrants it affected or another reason.

There are four marks for SPaG, so when you are checking through your exam paper in the last five minutes, it is important to look for any mistakes in spelling and grammar in your answer.

Practice

Use this page to continue your answer to Question 6.

Practice

Use this page to continue your answer to Question 6.

Sources booklet

Use these sources to answer the questions in Section A of the practice exam paper (see pages 40–42).

Source A: Two statements about the murder of Kelso Cochrane that were reported to the press by representatives of the Metropolitan Police. Both statements were made in the 48 hours after the murder in May 1959. The first was by Forbes-Leith, the leading detective on the case, and the second was by an unnamed senior police officer.

- The stabbing has absolutely nothing to do with racial conflict. The motive could have been robbery.

- We are satisfied that it was the work of a group of about six… white teenagers [who hated law and order and] who had only one motive in view – robbery or attempted robbery of a man who was walking the streets in the Notting Hill district alone in the early hours of the morning. The fact that he happens to be coloured does not, in our view, come into the question.

Source B: A photograph from June 1959, showing protesters marching outside the government buildings in Whitehall, London. The photograph was taken by a photographer working for an American media agency.

Remember!

In the exam, the sources will be in a separate sources booklet.

Answers

SUBJECT CONTENT

c800–c1500: Migration in medieval England

1. Medieval England

Your answers could include any **three** of:
- The land was ideal for farming and could support growing families and mass settlement.
- Mineral resources could be exported for profit or used by craftspeople to make goods for sale and profit.
- The lack of co-ordinated defences made invasion easy.
- The existing towns would be useful to take over and exploit as trading centres.
- There were existing well-established trade routes.

NB The question asks for 'invasion and settlement' not raiding.

2. Migration and settlement

Your **four** reasons could include:

Reasons for migration (any four)	Vikings	Normans	Jews	European workers	Italian bankers
To own/work England's fertile land	✓	✓			
For economic reasons – to make money, to trade, for job opportunities, etc.	✓	✓	✓	✓	✓
At the invitation of the monarch			✓		✓
As a result of being promised the throne		✓			
England was peaceful and stable				✓	

3. Migrants: Experience

Your answers could include any **four** of:
- Clashes with the Saxons, who wanted to claim back the Danelaw (Vikings)
- Opposition from the Saxons (Normans)
- Growth of anti-Semitism (Jews)
- Opposition from craft guilds (Weavers)
- Anti-foreigner opposition (Hansa merchants)

4. Migrants: Impact

Your answer could include **one** of the following similarities:
- Both impacted on language.
- Both developed towns.
- Both changed land ownership and replaced previous 'native' landowners.

Your answer could include **one** of the following differences:
- The Normans had a huge impact on the built environment through constructing stone buildings such as castles and cathedrals; the Vikings had less impact as they didn't build in stone.
- The Vikings established a system of government, whereas the Normans kept the Saxon system.
- The Normans changed the whole system of land ownership by introducing the feudal system.

5. York under the Vikings

Your answers could include three of:
- The population of York grew because of the number of migrants coming to the city.
- Hundreds of houses and workshops were built because the population of York grew.
- Skilled migrants coming to York needed workshops for their trades.
- The building of warehouses and wharves helped trade flourish.
- Trade flourished because skilled migrants made goods that were desired.
- As a multicultural city, York helped trade develop and flourish with the migrants' countries of origin.

c1500–c1700: Migration in early modern England

6. Early modern England

Your answers could include any two of:
- England became a Protestant country and welcomed Protestants fleeing Catholic persecution.
- The positive attitude of Parliament towards migrants enabled them to settle safely.
- The growth and development of trade made it likely that skilled workers would prosper.

7. Migration and settlement

For example:

There were several major changes in the reasons for migration in early modern England compared with medieval England. For the first time persecution became a major reason for migration to England. Those being persecuted, such as Huguenots, fled to England because they saw it as a place where they could live safely and practise their religion. People also came to England in this period because their employers took them there. For example, Indian ayahs came with the English families they worked for, and lascars came because they worked on ships transporting goods. However, others had very little choice. For example, some enslaved Africans were brought to England by their owners. None of these were reasons for migration to England in the medieval period.

8. Migrants: Experience

1. Huguenots
2. Your reasons could include any **two** of:
- The Huguenots had many skills but the Palatines did not.
- The Huguenots had friends and families in England to support them and the Palatines did not.

- The Huguenots came with money and/or quickly earned money in England, whereas the Palatines did not.
- The Palatines depended on charity to survive, and the Huguenots did not.

9. Migrants: Impact

Your answers could include any **two** of:
- The Huguenots boosted the cloth trade = created wealth for merchants and weavers, as well as for the Treasury through export taxes.
- The Huguenots boosted the fashion industry = created wealth for weavers, designers and seamstresses, as well as inspiring artists.
- The Huguenots kick-started industry = created incomes for the owners of the manufacturing industries, jobs for the workers and profits from exports.
- The Huguenots invested in the Bank of England = created a sound financial basis for economic growth.
- The Huguenots established London as a major financial centre = merchants working in England and those in Europe trusted London to invest their money.
- The Huguenots helped encourage religious toleration = society began to move towards being more tolerant of people who held different religious beliefs.

10. Sandwich and Canterbury

Your answer could include **one** of the following similarities:
- Both groups found work as weavers and produced high-quality cloth.
- Both groups were given a centre of their own by the city authorities.
- Both groups had economic success as they produced sought-after cloth.

Your answer could include **one** of the following differences:
- When the Walloons set up in other trades (not weaving), they were not in competition with existing trades in the area. The Flemish migrants were seen as being in competition with English people for jobs. They were fined for taking work if there was an English person who could take it.
- The Walloons created job opportunities for the English living in Canterbury by teaching them different skills. The Flemish migrants competed with English people for work.
- The Walloons developed their own community, based in the monastery they were given, and were not seen as a challenge to English-based facilities in Canterbury. The Flemish migrants in Sandwich didn't develop their own, separate community.
- The Walloons policed their own community and worked closely with the existing local officials. The Flemish migrants clashed with Sandwich officials.

11. The experience of the Huguenots

1. Your reasons could include any **three** of:
- The Huguenots were accepted by the English people living there.
- The Huguenots were skilled silk weavers who created a range of silk fabrics that sold well.
- The Huguenots taught their skills to English weavers and so avoided trouble.
- The Huguenots were supported by the monarchs William III and Mary II.
- The Huguenots had a good support network of their own.
- Some of the Huguenots were good businessmen.

2. Choose any reason as the most important but remember to justify your choice.

c1700–c1900: Migration in 18th- and 19th-century Britain

12. 18th- and 19th-century Britain

Your paragraph could include any **three** of the following:
- The growing numbers of factories offered work opportunities to migrants in Britain and overseas.
- The need to improve transport links and build docks offered work opportunities to migrants in Britain and from overseas.
- The freedom to express ideas that were unpopular or illegal encouraged migrants from overseas.
- The need for fewer agricultural workers encouraged internal migration as people lost their jobs or could not find work and moved elsewhere.

13. Migration and settlement

Your table could include the following reasons:

Reasons for migration from Ireland	Reasons for migration from India
• People had little choice but to migrate if they wanted to survive. • Britain was closest and therefore the easiest and cheapest place to get to. • There was a long history of migration between Britain and Ireland – people could join existing Irish communities in some cities. • Britain was also a stop-over on the way to North America or Australia.	• People came with their existing jobs, e.g. ayahs chose to stay with English families when those families returned to Britain. • Students wanted to go to British universities. • Princes preferred the government and freedoms of Britain. • Lascars came as part of their jobs transporting goods to Britain. Some chose to stay in search of better work and way of life.

14. Migrants: Experience

Your answer could include the following points:
The main problem faced by Asian migrants (ayahs and lascars) was that their employers abandoned them in England. They had few sought-after skills and many became destitute, forced to beg and/or rely on charity.

15. Migrants: Impact

Your map should include ideas such as:
- Political impact – some Irish migrants became involved in politics. For example, Feargus O'Connor was a leader in the Chartist movement.
- Economic impact
  - Many Irish migrants worked as navvies building the transport links that played a vital role in industry and trade.
  - Some Irish migrants owned and ran their own businesses, which contributed to Britain's economy.
- Impact on transport – the work of the Irish navvies meant that:
  - goods and raw materials could be transported
  - British towns and cities were better linked than before
  - people could travel far more and far more easily.
- Impact on urban environment – this was especially through work on the railways and canals that linked towns and cities.

16. Liverpool

Your answer could include **two** of the following advantages:
- job opportunities
- security of being part of a community of similar people
- the comfort of the catholic church.

Your answer could include **two** of the following disadvantages:
- poverty when work came to an end
- disease from living in poor overcrowded housing
- prejudice and resentment in the existing population.

17. Jewish migrants in London

Your answer could include the following points:
Sweatshops in Whitechapel were owned by Jews and many Jews worked in them. They were prepared to work long hours for low pay to produce clothes more cheaply than regular factories. Many English people in the area thought the Jews were taking work away from them.

c1900–present: Migration in modern Britain

18. Modern Britain

Your letter should include at least **one** reason, which might be:
- There was plenty of work available rebuilding Britain's infrastructure.
- The 1948 British Nationality Act gave people in the British colonies and former colonies the right to enter Britain and to stay.
- Having fought for Britain as a Commonwealth soldier, it made sense to migrate to Britain to find work and a better standard of life.

19. Migration and settlement

Your answer could include **one** of the following similarities:
- Both groups migrated to Britain to find work.
- Both groups migrated to settle and find a better life than in their home countries.

Your answer could include **one** of the following differences:
- Huguenots sought safety from persecution in a Protestant country. Persecution was not a factor for people from the Caribbean deciding to migrate.
- People from the Caribbean were recruited for specific jobs and invited to migrate by the government and other organisations. The Huguenots were not invited to migrate.

20. Migrants: Experience

For example:
The BUF (British Union of Fascists) was the first anti-immigration political party. It was particularly active during the 1930s and held anti-immigration marches. In 1936, one march turned into the Battle of Cable Street when fighting broke out between marchers, supporters of the Jewish community and the police. The BUF was disbanded in 1940 when Britain was at war with Germany, where Nazism had many things in common with fascism. However, in 1967, the National Front was founded. It was another group that opposed and campaigned against immigration. The National Front believed only white people should be British citizens. Anti-immigration groups were boosted by Enoch Powell's 'rivers of blood' speech where he criticised immigration. In 1982 the British National Party was founded. It was

another anti-immigrant group and held similar beliefs to the National Front. Members of these parties took part in the riots and violence that took place against immigrants throughout the period.

21. Migrants: Impact

Example answers are:

Transport:
Impact: They supplied labour to get transport going again after the Second World War.
Why important: This was important because the economy would not recover without transport to move people and goods.

NHS:
Impact: They supplied labour to enable the NHS to start properly in 1947 and to continue to staff the service afterwards.
Why important: This was important because, for the economy to flourish, the country needed its workforce to be kept healthy.

Industry:
Impact: They supplied labour to enable manufacturing, engineering and the textile industry to recover after the Second World War.
Why important: This was important for the recovery of the British economy because these are key industries.

22. Bristol

Your answer could include **two** of the following advantages:
- The Bristol Bus Boycott forced the Bristol Omnibus Company to end its colour bar. This showed migrants to be part of the city's workforce, helping them to integrate into the life of the city. In doing so, this helped to reduce racism.
- The St Paul's Festivals brought people from different ethnic communities together. This helped to increase understanding and tolerance, and so reduce racism.
- Various individuals worked to overcome racism. For example, Roy Hackett and Barbara Dettering who, through the WIDC, worked to reduce racism.

23. Asian migrants in Leicester

Your summary could include some of the following points:
Most Asian migrants to Leicester after 1945 found work and housing fairly easily. There were many jobs available and they also received support from other migrants. Additionally the city council was generally supportive. It allowed migrants to set up social and welfare clubs, and also to build mosques, gurdwaras and Hindu temples so they could continue their religious worship. Many Asian businessmen brought skills that enabled them to be successful in establishing businesses. These businesses served and employed local people, which in turn helped migrants to be accepted. Local people joined in the migrants' festivals and celebrations. However, Asian migrants did face discrimination in the same way as elsewhere. For example, many were underemployed. They also had to face the National Front anti-immigration protests in Leicester.

Notting Hill, c1948–c1970

24. Britain after 1945

Your answer could include any **three** of the following:
- There were jobs available rebuilding bombed houses, factories, offices and shops.

- To work in the NHS.
- To work in the new transport systems – London Transport and British Rail.
- The 1948 British Nationality Act made it possible for people from the Commonwealth to migrate to Britain.
- Migrants could earn at least three times more than they could in the Caribbean.
- Many in the Caribbean felt loyalty to Britain and wanted to help.

25. Notting Hill

Notting Hill landlords realised that, because of racial prejudice, there was a lack of rented housing for black people in London. Therefore, the landlords bought large but bomb-damaged houses cheaply in Notting Hill and rented them to Caribbean migrants, desperate for somewhere to live.

They applied for HMOs so that they could crowd as many migrants into each house as possible. The lack of rent controls meant that landlords could charge high rents for squalid rooms without improving or repairing the houses. They realised that the migrants were unlikely to complain about high rents and lack of repairs because they did not have anywhere else to go.

26. Caribbean cultures

Your answer could include the following points:
Food: Traders set up market stalls selling Caribbean food and ingredients. Also, business people set up pubs, cafes and restaurants that served Caribbean food. Examples include the 'Mangrove', the 'Apollo' and the 'El Rio'. This provided Caribbean migrants with access to food that was familiar to them and that they wanted. It also provided business opportunities and ways of meeting, socialising and getting support and help from others in the community.
Music: Caribbean migrants set up nightclubs that played Caribbean music, such as the 'Metro Club'. Others held 'shebeens' where they could listen to Caribbean music in their homes or empty buildings. The Basing Street Studios produced Caribbean music so it became more readily available. These provided ways for Caribbean migrants to continue to listen to and develop their own music as well as ways of meeting and socialising with others in the community. It also provided business opportunities for some migrants.

27. Racism and policing

Your answer could include any **three** of the following:
- The police were racist.
- Violent anti-immigration groups were based in Notting Hill.
- The Caribbean community didn't trust the police.
- Police failure to find the murderers of Kelso Cochrane led the black community to believe they had to fight for civil rights themselves.
- Police failure to describe the 1958 riots and the murder of Kelso Cochrane as racially motivated showed Notting Hill residents that the police didn't understand the community.

28. Black activism

Your answer could include the following points:
In the 1950s newspapers were one of the few ways of sharing ideas and distributing information in a local area. The 'West Indian Gazette' gave Caribbean people in Notting Hill somewhere where they could express and share their ideas and tell others about their experiences. It was therefore a vital way of giving Caribbean people a voice and gave them information and ideas which helped them. It helped give the Caribbean people in Notting Hill a sense of identity.

PRACTICE

39. Practice

1. Your answer could include any **two** of the following:
- They were formed to fight racial equality (1) like the Black Panthers in the USA (1).
- They were founded in 1968 (1), as part of the protest movement that followed the 1958 riots (1).
- They campaigned against police brutality (1) because the police in London had a reputation for treating black people aggressively (1).
- They campaigned about social issues (1), such as housing and employment for black people (1).
- They encouraged black people to have pride in their community and identity (1) by promoting black history and culture (1).

40. Practice

2. (a) Your answer could include some of the following relevant points.

Source A: It is useful because it summarises the official police response, which denied that the murder was racially motivated. It is also useful as a public statement that shows how the police officially treated the murder. The police did not wish to cause further riots in Notting Hill, such as those of 1958, so this could explain the determination to deny the racial link.

It is less useful in showing whether the police really thought that the murder was racially motivated. They would have avoided publicising any evidence supporting this fact since they would not have wanted to cause panic or further violence in Notting Hill. Also, it was published 48 hours after the murder, when tensions were at a high point. So it cannot reflect the full findings of the investigation, which led to the Home Secretary starting a government investigation into race relations.

Source B: It is useful because it shows that in June 1959, one month after the murder, there were protesters outside government buildings. This shows the significance of the murder in the community. It is also useful as a good example of the anger felt within the black community of Notting Hill – many people believed that the murder was racially motivated and that it had not been handled properly by the police. It also shows that the protests about the murder were widely enough known for a photojournalist to take a photo.

It is less useful because the picture offers a limited view, so it is difficult to assess the scale of the protest beyond the four people seen. It is also less useful because it was taken by a photojournalist. They may have selected the scene to generate media interest, rather than to be representative. Another reason why this source is less useful is that it is not representative of the way the murder was presented in the general media, such as in the 'Daily Mirror', which ran the headline 'It was not a racial killing'.

42. Practice

2. (b) For example:

Detail in Source B that I would follow up: There are four people protesting the murder.

Question I would ask: How many people were involved in the protests about the murder?

What type of source I could use: Police briefing records for officers on the beat near the Whitehall government offices.

How this might help my question: They would probably contain notes to inform the police officers of the size of the protests seen while patrolling near the buildings.

43. Practice

3. Your answer could include the following relevant differences:
- Huguenots were supported by English monarchs Charles II and William and Mary; Jewish migrants received no such support by the British government in the 19th century.
- Huguenots were welcomed in by relatives who had been successfully settled in England, and accepted into English society, for many years; although the settled Jewish community offered support to newer Jewish migrants, some Jews were wary of them – they were concerned their arrival would worsen the treatment of Jews already settled in Britain, who already faced anti-Semitism.
- Many Huguenots had skills that were welcomed in England and they quickly found skilled work, often in family businesses; many Jewish migrants were unable to find skilled work and had to resort to unskilled labour in sweatshops, for example in Whitechapel.
- The religious beliefs and worship of the Huguenots were respected as they were similar to English Protestantism; Jewish migrants often faced anti-Semitic responses to their religious practices and beliefs.

44. Practice

4. Your answer could include the following points:
- Flemish and Dutch migrants to Britain, such as the families who settled in Sandwich and Canterbury in the 1500s before moving to other towns and cities, boosted the cloth industry. Good cloth was a luxury item which could be sold for high prices in Britain and abroad.
- Huguenot settlers in the 1600s developed silk weaving in Britain, and Spitalfields in London became famous for silk cloth. Most of the silk was exported, which boosted British trade.
- Many migrants, especially the Huguenots, invested in the Bank of England in 1684. This was important in improving the British economy, for example in allowing the government to borrow money and making London a centre for international trade.
- Skilled migrants helped develop the iron and paper industries in Britain, which helped Britain turn into a manufacturing nation.
- British explorers and colonisers had opened up trading routes and they began to create the British Empire, which gave Britain access to wealth and exotic trade items.
- Global trading companies, such as the Royal African Company in the 1660s, increased British international trade. This included the transatlantic slave trade, which enslaved huge numbers of Africans in order to make large profits for British investors.

47–55. Practice

5. Answers must make a judgement about how far the student agrees with the statement. Evidence to support the statement includes:
- Viking raiding parties, who were in Britain to fight and plunder, would set up temporary settlements so that they could continue raiding when the better weather arrived.
- Many Vikings in the late 9th century arrived with the Viking Great Army hoping to capture land.
- In 1066 Norman invaders arrived, which led to the subsequent conquest and settlement of England.

Evidence against the statement includes:
- To settle on conquered land: Many Scandinavian and Norman settlers came to Britain after the Viking and Norman invasions to settle land that had already been conquered.
- To trade and lend money: In the 11th century, Jewish merchants came to England to work as merchants and moneylenders, and in the 13th century, Christian bankers and merchants migrated from northern Italy to make money by trading and lending money.
- To find work: Migrants arrived from Europe looking for labouring work, especially after the Black Death of 1348–51. Skilled workers migrated to south-east England from northern Europe looking for work.
- By invitation from the monarch: William I invited Jewish moneylenders to migrate to support him financially; and, from 1270, English monarchs encouraged skilled weavers to settle in England.

6. Answers must make a judgement about how far the student agrees with the statement. Evidence to support the statement includes:
- In the 18th and 19th centuries, many Irish immigrants lived in poor, run-down areas of cities such as Liverpool. Typhus, a disease caused by poor living conditions, became known as 'Irish fever' because of the number of Irish immigrants who caught the disease as a result of their poor living conditions.
- Many Jewish immigrants in the 19th century ended up in areas such as Spitalfields and Whitechapel in overcrowded housing conditions. Many were homeless or relied on workhouses and slum housing.
- Until the 1968 Race Relations Act, landlords in some areas refused to accept immigrants as tenants, forcing them to seek low-quality accommodation in areas like Notting Hill; after 1968, this discrimination continued but unofficially.

Evidence against the statement includes:
- Poor working conditions: Jewish and Irish immigrants in the 18th and 19th centuries often had to find work that was physically challenging and frequently dangerous, e.g. as 'navvies', in sweatshops and factories, and on the docks.
- Racial tensions led to violence and protests by British nationalists: e.g. attacks on Jewish families in Whitechapel in the 19th century, and riots in Notting Hill in 1958 and in Bradford, Oldham and Burnley in 2001.
- Opposition from workers and unions over employment: e.g. clothing factory owners opposed sweatshops, which employed immigrants in the 19th century, and in 1918, immigrant port workers faced riots when soldiers returning from the First World War protested against immigrants who were employed in the jobs that they wanted.
- Legal challenges: e.g. challenges caused by the 1962 Commonwealth Immigrants Act which limited migrants' rights to settle in Britain; and the difficulties of the 'Windrush generation', who had difficulty providing legal proof of status after 2012.

Published by Pearson Education Limited, 80 Strand, London, WC2R 0RL.

www.pearsonschoolsandfecolleges.co.uk

Copies of official specifications for all Pearson qualifications may be found on the website: qualifications.pearson.com

Text, audio and illustrations © Pearson Education Limited 2022
Typeset and illustrated by Florence Production Ltd
Produced by Florence Production Ltd
Cover illustration by Kamae Design Limited

The rights of Rosemary Rees and Ben Armstrong to be identified as authors of this work has been asserted by them in accordance with the Copyright, Designs and Patents Act 1988.

First published 2022
25 24
10 9 8 7

British Library Cataloguing in Publication Data
A catalogue record for this book is available from the British Library

ISBN 978 1 292 40631 2

Printed in Great Britain by Bell and Bain Ltd, Glasgow

Acknowledgements
The publisher would like to thank the following for their kind permission to reproduce their photographs:

Alamy Stock Photo: Lakeview Images 8, The Picture Art Collection 8, Granger Historical Picture Archive 9, Robert Evans 11, Granger Historical Picture Archive 15, The Print Collector/Heritage-Images 16, PA Images 20, Museum of London/Heritage-Images 21, David Warren 23, Chronicle 24, Keystone Pictures USA/ZUMA Press 56; **Bridgeman Art Library Limited**: Look and Learn 10; **Getty Images**: duncan1890 7, Duncan1890/DigitalVision Vectors 15, Evening Standard/Hulton Archive 26, FPG/Archive Photos 28, Hulton Deutsch/Corbis Historical 32; **Michiel Jansz. van Mierevelt**: Michiel Jansz. van Mierevelt (1567–1641) 9; **Wellcome Collection**: Wellcome Collection available under Creative Commons CC-PD 17.

Text
Page 32: **The People Newspaper:** Extract from 'Rachman: These Are The Facts', *The People* 14 July 1963. Author: Peter Forbes, pp. 2–3. Page 56: **Zero Books:** Extract from *Murder in Notting Hill*, by Mark Olden, Zero Books, 2011, p. 47. Page 56: **Metropolitan Police:** Anonymous source, Metropolitan Police, 1959. Source: *Murder in Notting Hill*, by Mark Olden, Zero Books, 2011, p. 47. Page 56: **Metropolitan Police:** Attributed to Detective Superintendent Ian Forbes Leith, Metropolitan Police, 1959. Source: *Murder in Notting Hill*, by Mark Olden, Zero Books, 2011, p. 47.

Notes from the publisher
1. While the publishers have made every attempt to ensure that advice on the qualification and its assessment is accurate, the official specification and associated assessment guidance materials are the only authoritative source of information and should always be referred to for definitive guidance.

Pearson examiners have not contributed to any sections in this resource relevant to examination papers for which they have responsibility.

2. Pearson has robust editorial processes, including answer and fact checks, to ensure the accuracy of the content in this publication, and every effort is made to ensure this publication is free of errors. We are, however, only human, and occasionally errors do occur. Pearson is not liable for any misunderstandings that arise as a result of errors in this publication, but it is our priority to ensure that the content is accurate. If you spot an error, please do contact us at resourcescorrections@pearson.com so we can make sure it is corrected.